Tastes of
CLEMSON
BLUE CHEESE

By Christian Thormose

CLEMSON
UNIVERSITY
PRESS

Clemson University Press
Director | *John Morgenstern*
Managing Editor | *Alison Mero*

Design Consultant
Dirt Road Media
Editor | *Chasiti Kirkland Jackson*
Graphic Designer | *Jamie Pearson*

Photographers
Bloom Photography | *Haley Dunbar Mitchell*
FireMedia | *John Robeson*
Clemson University Staff Photographer | *Jenni Tonkin*

Food Stylists
Jill Norton Leopard
Susan Soonok Watkins

We also extend a special thanks to *Tindall Construction*
for the use of its beautifully decorated home and well-appointed kitchen.

ISBN 978-1-942954-58-3

Published by Clemson University Press
Printed by Ingram/Lightning Source

For copies, contact Clemson University Press: 116 Sigma Drive, Clemson, SC 29634 or order online at www.clemson.edu/press.

Dedicated to:
The people who love to teach and the people who are dedicated to learning

Acknowledgments:
I appreciate all the people who made this book possible,
especially John Morgenstern and Alison Mero at Clemson University Press,
who had the guts to take on this project.

To Scott Pigeon, Master Cheesemaker Anthony P. Pounders,
and his entire staff:
Thanks for your hard work and dedication required to
create the wonderful Clemson Blue Cheese.

Bon appétit and warm wishes

Contents

Clemson Blue Cheese

At Clemson, we believe knowledge should be revealed, explored, and passed on. In that tradition, as a chef at the university, I'm passing on the secrets I've learned about another school tradition, Clemson Blue Cheese. The textbook is this cookbook — 200 recipes that feature the versatile delicacy developed here, perfected here, still made here, and used in campus kitchens, dining halls, restaurants, and food courts. You'll also find Clemson Blue Cheese in some restaurants around this university town. Maybe in your town, too.

Throughout much of the South and the nation, Clemson means football. To the university's faithful, Clemson also stands for its signature blue cheese. Clemson Blue Cheese dates back to the 1940s, when a college professor first cured it in an abandoned railroad tunnel near Walhalla, S.C. It has legions of fans in these parts, but to the rest of the nation, Clemson Blue Cheese remains largely unknown.

If you're among those unfamiliar with Clemson Blue Cheese, maybe some recipes in this cookbook will convert you. Admittedly, blue cheese is America's least favorite. But ours tastes surprisingly "different," a word used by many who finally try it. Clemson Blue Cheese is creamy, not too pungent, and the perfect blend of sweet and salty. It is content whipped into mashed potatoes, stirred into grits, crumbled on steak, stuffed into mushrooms, and added to dozens of other dishes that score big with fans.

Our blue cheese has won national awards and is still winning them. Hopefully, it's also a winner with you. Out of 200 recipes, I'm sure you'll find something to love. Enjoy!

ITS ORIGIN

In November 1853, Blue Ridge Railroad workers started a tunnel through Stumphouse Mountain in Oconee County. Plans called for it to connect the Midwest to the bustling port of Charleston.

Financial difficulties in 1859 halted the project, however. By then, more than $1 million had been spent, and the South Carolina Legislature voted to stop funding it. Efforts to restart construction failed when the Civil War began, and Stumphouse Mountain Tunnel was abandoned. The partially completed portion remained unused until 1940, when Clemson professor, Dr. P. G. Miller, realized the tunnel's high humidity and almost constant temperature would likely cure blue cheese. The tunnel also had many of the same characteristics as the caves used to make Roquefort cheese in France. After experiments to ensure mold grew in the tunnel, the Clemson A&M College dairy made its first batch of blue cheese on Jan. 17, 1941. From campus, the cheese was transported 30 miles to Stumphouse Tunnel, where it aged. Milk from the college's dairy cows was used to make the very first batch of Clemson Blue Cheese. Fifteen pounds was sent to the tunnel that day — the first time blue cheese was made in the South. Other than a gap in production during World War II (milk was rationed for aviation cadets stationed on campus), Clemson Blue Cheese aged in Stumphouse Tunnel until construction in 1956 of a campus facility that replicated the tunnel's high humidity and temperature.

PRODUCTION

In a small, spotless cheese room, production starts before the milk arrives. The process begins by making buttermilk from skim milk and a cheese culture.

The milk must contain at least 3.4% butterfat and is tested on campus. Milk quality significantly affects clotting, production time and the firmness of curds. First, milk is poured into a 300-gallon vat and gradually heated to 72 degrees. Next, buttermilk is added to start production and help firm curd particles. The enzyme, Capalase, removes hydrogen peroxide from the milk prior to actual cheese making. From here, the milk is heated to 89 degrees. Next, mold and rennet are added. The blue mold,

heat is then increased to 100 degrees for 1½ hours. From here, cheese master Anthony Pounders turns science into art. By feeling the firmness of the curds, he determines the exact moment to stop the heating process.

Once curds reach the right firmness, they are pumped out of the vat, salted, and poured into perforated hoops. For four consecutive hours, workers flip the cheese every 20 minutes. Afterward, they cover it with cheesecloth, and let it dry overnight at room temperature. The next day, the cheese is "un-hooped," salted and kept in a humidity-controlled cooler. After two days, the cheese is again rolled in salt. On day six, the cheese is dipped in a mold inhibitor, bagged and poked with 100 long needles, a necessary step that allows air to reach inside the cheese. This encourages "good" mold to grow when the *Penicillum roqueforti* gets oxygen and begins making blue mold.

After five weeks, workers scrape the cheese and store it in a vacuum bag. From there,

U.S. CHAMPIONSHIP CHEESE CONTEST

Clemson University has found a recipe for success with its blue cheese, which claimed fourth spot in its class at the 2019 U.S. Championship Cheese Contest. Team Amick's Choice scored 97.05 out of 100 possible points with its entry Mild Blue Cheese Batch No. 6. Only tenths of points separated the top four finishers. Entries from 35 states were evaluated during the two-day competition in Green Bay, Wisconsin.

Penicillum roqueforti, ripens and flavors blue cheese. Rennet, found in the stomach lining of mammals, coagulates milk, and separates it into curds. The mold and rennet are blended thoroughly into the milk, and the mixture is left to set for one to two hours.

When the curd reaches a custard-like consistency, it is cut horizontally and vertically into small pieces to expel whey. The

the cheese is kept in a 38-degree cooler for four months. In the final stages of cheese making, Pounders and his team scrape the cheese again, and slice it into wheels and wedges. Pieces that don't reach optimal weight are sold as crumbles. Aging Clemson Blue Cheese is a six-month process, but the final result is well worth the effort. Experts the world over have recognized Clemson Blue for its high quality and craftsmanship.

To order Clemson Blue Cheese products, visit clemsonbluecheese.com, where you'll find hoops, wheels, wedges, dressing and krumbles — our version of crumbles.

ABOUT THE CHEESEMAKER: ANTHONY POUNDERS

A handful of universities continue to make cheese as part of their agriculture and dairy science programs. Clemson is the only school in the South that makes blue cheese. In 2009, its cheese ranked among the best in the nation, scoring highly with judges during the 15th biennial U.S. Championship Cheese Contest in Green Bay, Wisconsin. Clemson Blue Cheese dates back to 1940, when a university dairy professor cured the cheese in the damp air of Stumphouse Mountain Tunnel near Walhalla, S.C. Production was moved in 1958 to Clemson's Newman Hall, where air-conditioned ripening rooms replicate the temperature and humidity of an unfinished railroad tunnel.

Today, cheese master Anthony Pounders makes cheese the old-school way. One 600-gallon vat turns out about 550 pounds

"And I'm still learning," Pounders says. "It's a never-ending process when you're dealing with cheese."

of cheese, which is salted, bagged and aged six months. Once ready, he scrapes and packages the cheese by hand, a painstaking but necessary process. Pounders started at Clemson milking cows. Now, he is responsible for making its blue cheese, which he has done for more than 25 years.

Clemson Blue Cheese

Once home with Clemson Blue Cheese, wrap it well and refrigerate in an airtight container. Proper storage prevents the cheese from tainting other foods and keeps the blue cheese from taking on additional food flavors. Stored well, blue cheese keeps flawlessly in the refrigerator for two to three weeks. Refrigerated cheese continues to mature, get creamier and develop a mellower flavor. For extended storage, blue cheese also freezes well. When properly covered in cling wrap, then rolled in freezer paper, and stored in heavy-duty freezer bags, blue cheese keeps up to three months.

Blue cheese is tastier when served at room temperature.

Once frozen, slowly defrost blue cheese in the refrigerator, typically, two to three days. This prevents the cheese from getting too crumbly.

Once blue cheese is defrosted, it should be eaten within a week and not refrozen.

Frozen blue cheese shreds easily. Remove a piece from the freezer, shred what's needed, and return the rest. Blue cheese, much like red wine, is tastier when served at room temperature. For maximum flavor, remove cheese from the refrigerator at least one hour before serving. Discard blue cheese if it tastes rancid or has mold not native to the manufacturing process.

A BLUE CHEESE EVEN SKEPTICS WILL LOVE

Clemson Blue is delightfully bold, yet reserved, with a slight peppery note and layers of flavor. Its clean, sweet finish makes it ideal for cooking, crumbling, or eating out of hand. It should always be the centerpiece of any cheeseboard or display.

Extremely versatile, Clemson Blue Cheese goes well with:
- Cheese dips and dressings
- Risotto, pastas, and pizza
- Crumbled over steaks and burgers
- Blended into mashed potatoes
- Crumbled on salads
- Spread on crostini with chopped dates, dried apricots or olives
- Mixed into potato salad or pasta salad

Like every blue cheese, Clemson Blue is naturally salty — the very reason many recipes in this book do not include salt. Always taste the finished product, however, and add seasoning when needed. Sometimes, a dash of salt accentuates other flavors and brings everything together in perfect balance.

> Clemson Blue Cheese should always be the centerpiece of any breadboard or display.

PAIRS WELL WITH EVERY OCCASION

Experts often disagree about what wine pairs well Clemson Blue, mainly because it's one of the most flavorful blue cheeses. Most recommend full-bodied reds, such as Hermitage, Zinfandel, Barolo, Gevrey-Chambertin, Cabernet Sauvignon, St. Émilion, or Chianti Classico. Those who disagree think Clemson Blue is too salty for red wine or that its pungent aroma and creaminess makes red wine taste bitter. Often, those folks choose champagne or sparkling wine.

Just as many prefer white wine. Some experts recommend a full-bodied variety like Meursault and Sauternes, while those who like something fruity choose Chenin Blanc or Sauvignon Blanc. If sweet whites or desserts wines suit you better, try Muscat, Sauterne, Gewürztraminer or Late Harvest Riesling.

Too many choices? Don't worry. Nearly everyone agrees that tawny ports, vintage ports, dry sherry, cognac, and armagnac pair well with Clemson Blue Cheese. Most beers do not. Exceptions are dark, yeasty micro-brews.

I say ignore the "experts," experiment at your leisure, and discover the countless ways to enjoy Clemson Blue Cheese. ■

LET'S START COOKING

Recipes in this book include:
- The name of the dish
- The number of servings the recipe provides (yield)
- Ingredients and how much to use
- Preparation and techniques

Before you start cooking, read each recipe entirely, have all the ingredients on hand, and pay attention to the time needed to complete the recipe.

Recipes

WEIGHT AND MEASUREMENTS OF CLEMSON BLUE CHEESE CRUMBLES

1/4 ounce = 1 tablespoon
1/2 ounce = 2 tablespoons
1 ounce = 1/4 cup
2 ounces = 1/2 cup
4 ounces = 1 cup
8 ounces = 2 cups (1 pint)
16 ounces = 4 cups (1 quart)

TASTES OF CLEMSON BLUE CHEESE

Appetizers

Potato Pancakes with Clemson Blue Cheese on Mesclun Greens
Servings: 6

1 Tbsp	Sherry vinegar or balsamic vinegar	1 small	Garlic clove, minced
½ tsp	Dijon mustard	4 Tbsp	Chives or scallion tops, chopped
1¾ tsp	Salt	1½ pound	Baking potatoes (about 3)
3 Tbsp	Sour cream	6 ounces	Clemson Blue Cheese, crumbled
1 Tbsp	Olive oil	4 ounces	Mesclun greens (about 1½ quarts)
1 Tbsp	Minced shallots	Fresh ground black pepper	

DRESSING:
In a large bowl, combine vinegar, mustard, ¼ teaspoon of salt, and a pinch of pepper. Add sour cream, whisking. Stir in shallots, garlic, and 2 tablespoons of chives. Set dressing aside.

HORS D'OEVRES:
Peel potatoes and grate. Squeeze excess liquid from the potatoes. Stir in the remaining 1½ teaspoons of salt and ⅛ teaspoon of pepper. Brush a large non-stick frying pan with some of the oil. You may need to use 2 pans. Use half of the grated potatoes to make 6 piles in the pan, and press them into flat cakes about 2½ inches in diameter. Top each round of potatoes with ⅙ of the Clemson Blue Cheese and 1 teaspoon of chives. Press the remaining grated potatoes onto the blue cheese so that the cheese is completely covered.

In a pan over moderate heat, cook potatoes until they form a crust on the bottom (about 1 minute). Reduce the heat to low, and cook the potato cakes until they are lightly browned on the bottom (about 10 minutes). Flip each potato cake. Continue cooking until the potatoes are cooked through (about 12 minutes longer). Just before the potato cakes are done, toss the salad with the dressing. Divide the greens among 6 plates, and place hot potato cakes on the greens.

Clemson Blue Cheese Stuffed Mushrooms
Servings: 6 / Yield: 24

24 large	Mushrooms, cleaned	8 ounces	Cream cheese
2 ounces	Butter	3 ounces	Clemson Blue Cheese, crumbled
1 medium	Onion, chopped	3 Tbsp	Sherry
2 cloves	Garlic, minced	Salt and pepper	
¼ cup	Chopped parsley		

Remove stems from mushrooms. Chop stems and set aside. Melt butter in a large sauté pan; add onions and garlic; and sauté for 1 minute. Add chopped mushroom stems and sauté for another 3 minutes. Add parsley, cream cheese, and Clemson Blue Cheese. Stir until cheeses are melted; add sherry and salt and pepper to taste. Spoon the cheese mixture into mushroom caps, and place them in an ovenproof dish or on a sheet pan. Bake in a 375-degree oven for 10 minutes or until mushrooms are cooked and cheeses are light brown.

Portobello Mushrooms with Clemson Blue Cheese
Servings: 4

2 Tbsp	Butter	2 Tbsp	White wine
4 large	Portobello mushrooms	2 Tbsp	Olive oil
2	Roasted red bell peppers	½ cup	Clemson Blue Cheese, crumbled
½ tsp	Ground pepper	1 Tbsp	Chopped parsley

In a large sauté pan, melt butter. Slice mushrooms into ½-inch strips, and sauté in the melted butter over medium heat for 5 to 6 minutes. Sprinkle with ground pepper.

In a food processor, purée roasted red bell peppers with white wine and olive oil.
Place mushrooms on salad plates; pour roasted red pepper purée over them; and top with Clemson Blue Cheese and parsley.

Salmon, Green Peas, and Clemson Blue Cheese Cakes
Servings: 8

2 Tbsp	Butter	3	Eggs
1 large	Onion, finely chopped	1 Tbsp	Lemon juice
1 stalk	Celery, finely chopped	1 tsp	Salt
1 pound	Salmon, cooked	½ tsp	Cayenne
5 ounces	Cream cheese, cubed	1½ cups	Green peas
4 ounces	Clemson Blue Cheese, crumbled	4 cups	Bread crumbs

Heat butter in a large sauté pan over moderate heat. Sauté onions and celery until onions are translucent (about 2 minutes). Add salmon and stir until it breaks into small pieces. Add cream cheese and Clemson Blue Cheese, and cook until cheeses are almost melted. Remove the pan from the heat and add eggs, one at the time. Add lemon juice, salt, and cayenne pepper. Stir in peas. Add 2 cups of bread crumbs and mix well. Form into 8 patties and press both sides of each into the remaining bread crumbs. Pan-fry or deep-fry until golden brown. TIP: Serve with Cajun rémoulade, tartar sauce, or herbed mayonnaise.

Clemson Blue Cheese Puffs
Yield: 24 / Servings: 6

¼ cup	Butter	3 large	Eggs
¾ cup	Water	4 ounces	Clemson Blue Cheese
¾ cup	All-purpose flour	pinch	Nutmeg

In a heavy sauce pan, bring butter and water to a boil. Remove from the heat, and whisk in flour. When well combined, stir in eggs, one at a time, and then Clemson Blue Cheese and nutmeg. Using a tablespoon, drop dough (2 inches apart) onto buttered baking sheet and bake at 375F for 25 to 30 minutes or until golden brown.

Pecan Clemson Blue Cheese Crackers

Servings: 15 / Yield: 30

4 ounces	Butter, softened	1 Tbsp	Milk
8 ounces	Clemson Blue Cheese, crumbled	1	Egg, beaten
1½ cups	Flour	⅓ cup	Pecans, finely chopped
1 tsp	Ground white pepper		

In a mixing bowl, combine butter and Clemson Blue Cheese, mixing until smooth. Add flour and pepper and mix until it is in large crumbles. Add milk and egg and mix until combined.

On a floured board, press the dough into a ball and then roll it into a 12-inch long log. Spread the pecans on the board and roll the log in it to cover the outside of the log. Wrap in plastic and refrigerate for a minimum of 2 hours.

Cut the log in ⅜-inch slices and place them on a lightly greased baking sheet (1 inch apart). Bake in a 350-degree oven for 20 to 22 minutes until barely browned.

Rice and Clemson Blue Cheese Crisps

Servings: 8 / Yield: 8

1 cup	Basmati rice	½ cup	Clemson Blue Cheese
¼ cup	Wild rice	1 tsp	Ground white pepper
1 cup	Parmesan cheese, grated		

In a large pot, bring 6 cups water to a boil, and add basmati and wild rice; cover and simmer for about 1 hour until rice is very soft. Chill.

In a food processor, blend rice and add cheeses and pepper. Place ½ cup of rice mixture on a greased baking sheet; spread it out and shape into thin, 8 inch-rounds. Continue with remaining rice mixture. Bake rounds in a 450-degree oven until golden brown and crisp (about 10 minutes).

Spicy Sweet Potato Chips

Servings: 4

2 large	Sweet potatoes, peeled	1 tsp	Salt
1 tsp	Cayenne pepper powder	½ tsp	Ground cumin
1 tsp	Chili powder	½ tsp	Ground white pepper
1 tsp	Granulated garlic		

Cut sweet potatoes lengthwise into thin, long slices, and place in a large bowl of ice water. Chill for 1 hour. In a small mixing bowl, combine cayenne, chili, garlic, salt, cumin, and pepper. Drain sweet potato slices and pat dry on paper towels. Heat oil to 375F and fry in a single layer until golden brown (about 2 to 3 minutes). Drain on paper towels, and sprinkle with spice mixture.
TIP: Serve with Clemson Blue Cheese and Chive Dip (see pg. 16).

Clemson Blue Cheese Finger Sandwiches with Honey
Servings: 6

4 ounces	Clemson Blue Cheese, crumbled	½ cup	Walnuts, toasted and chopped
4 ounces	Cream cheese	⅓ cup	Honey
1 loaf	Raisin bread		

In a food processor or mixing bowl, combine Clemson Blue Cheese and cream cheese. Cut bread into ¼-inch slices, and spread each slice with a small amount of cheese mixture. Sprinkle walnuts on top and drizzle with honey. Cut each slice in half and arrange on a serving platter.

Clemson Blue Cheese Fondue
Servings: 6

2 Tbsp	Butter	2 cups	Heavy cream
2 tsp	Thyme, chopped	2 cups	Clemson Blue Cheese, crumbled
2 tsp	Garlic, finely chopped	1 tsp	Ground white pepper
2 Tbsp	White wine		

In a small sauce pot, melt butter and add thyme and garlic; cook slowly until the garlic is soft, but not brown (about 2 minutes). Add white wine and reduce by ½. Add heavy cream and reduce by ⅓. Remove the sauce pot from the heat. Add the blue cheese and stir until cheese is melted and the mixture is smooth. Add pepper and pour into a fondue pot over low heat. **TIP: Serve with cubed bread, vegetables, or fruit.**

Clemson Blue Cheese Wafers
Servings: 12

4 ounces	Clemson Blue Cheese, crumbled	1	egg yolk
4 ounces	butter, softened	1 cup	flour

In a mixing bowl, combine Clemson Blue Cheese, butter, and egg yolk, and blend well. Fold in flour. Roll mixture in aluminum foil, plastic wrap, or parchment paper, and refrigerate 2 to 3 hours. Cut into slices a little more than ¼-inch thick. Bake on baking sheet at 425F for 15 minutes or until golden brown.

Clemson Blue Cheese and Pecan Ham Roll
Servings: 8

6 ounces	Unsalted butter, room temperature	¼ cup	Chopped pecans
6 ounces	Clemson Blue Cheese, crumbled	2 Tbsp	Sherry
4 ounces	Boursin cheese	2 pounds	Buffet ham, thinly sliced

In a mixing bowl, combine butter, Clemson Blue Cheese, and Boursin cheese; add pecans and sherry. Spread cheese mixture on ham slices and roll lengthwise.

Clemson Blue Cheese Walnut Ball
Servings: 20

16 ounces	Cream cheese, softened	1 tsp	Paprika
8 ounces	Clemson Blue Cheese, crumbled	1 tsp	Crushed red pepper flakes
½ cup	Celery, finely chopped	12 ounces	Walnut, chopped
¼ cup	Green onions, finely chopped		

In a mixing bowl, combine cream cheese, Clemson Blue Cheese, celery, green onions, paprika, and red pepper flakes. Form into 2 cheese balls. Roll each cheese ball in walnuts, covering entire surface. Refrigerate for several hours. Serve surrounded by crackers or toast.

Salami Cones with Clemson Blue Cheese
Servings: 10 / Yield: 30 cones

15	Salami, thinly sliced	4 ounces	Boursin cheese
4 ounces	Clemson Blue Cheese	2 Tbsp	Dry sherry

Cut salami slices in half and twist each into a cone, pressing the edges together. In a food processor or mixing bowl, combine Clemson Blue Cheese and Boursin cheese, add sherry, and blend until smooth. With a pastry bag, fill the cones with the cheese mixture. Chill at least 1 hour before serving.

Clemson Blue Cheese Balls
Servings: 4

2 ounces	Butter	½ cup	All-purpose flour
½ cup	Clemson Blue Cheese	⅔ cup	Chopped pecans

In a mixing bowl, combine butter and Clemson Blue Cheese, mix in flour, and blend well; add pecans. Roll mixture into walnut-sized balls, and bake on baking sheet at 350F for 15 minutes.

Clemson Blue Cheese Dip
Servings: 6

1⅓ pound	Clemson Blue Cheese	⅓ cup	Heavy cream
16 ounces	Cream cheese	⅔ tsp	Salt
⅓ large	Red onion, diced	⅔ tsp	White pepper
⅓ Tbsp	Granulated garlic	⅓ cup	Carrots, shredded and blanched

Mix all ingredients together in a mixer, using the paddle. Scoop into oval serving dishes (7 ounces per dish). Bake in a 375-degree oven until bubbly at the edges and heated through. TIP: Serve each dish with 3 pieces of grilled pita bread.

Clemson Blue Cheese Dip with Brandy and Pecans
Servings: 6

5 ounces	Clemson Blue Cheese, crumbled	2 tsp	Worcestershire sauce
4 ounces	Cream cheese, softened	2 Tbsp	Brandy
2 ounces	Butter, softened	½ cup	Pecans, chopped
¼ cup	Mayonnaise		

In a mixing bowl, beat together Clemson Blue Cheese, cream cheese, and butter. Add mayonnaise, Worcestershire, and brandy, and beat until smooth. Mix in pecans. Spoon mixture into a bowl. Refrigerate for at least 1 hour before serving. TIP: Serve with crackers, pita bread, or melba toast, and fresh fruit and berries.

Clemson Blue Cheese Dip with Bacon and Walnuts
Served warm / Servings: 12

¼ cup	Walnuts, chopped	⅓ cup	Sour cream
8	Bacon slices, diced	6 ounces	Clemson Blue Cheese
2 tsp	Garlic, chopped	2 Tbsp	Chives, chopped
14 ounces	Cream cheese	1 Tbsp	White pepper

Heat oven to 350F. Spread walnuts in a single layer on a baking sheet, and bake in oven until lightly toasted. Cook bacon in a skillet until crisp. Spoon bacon into a strainer, leaving about 1 tablespoon of bacon grease in the skillet; add garlic and sauté until lightly browned (about 1 minute). In a mixing bowl, combine cream cheese with sour cream and beat until smooth. Stir in bacon, garlic, Clemson Blue Cheese, chives, and white pepper.

Spoon mixture into a 1-quart baking dish or four 1-cup baking dishes, and bake in oven for 15 to 25 minutes or until bubbly and golden brown. Sprinkle with toasted walnuts.

Veggie Dip
Servings: 12 / Yield: 3 cups

1 cup	Dried tart cherries, chopped	1 cup	Sour cream
½ cup	Clemson Blue Cheese, crumbled	¼ cup	Mayonnaise
½ cup	Walnuts, chopped		

In a medium bowl, combine cherries, Clemson Blue Cheese, and walnuts. Stir in sour cream and mayonnaise; mix well. Chill about 1 hour to blend flavors. Serve with celery, carrots, cauliflower, cucumber, broccoli, and green or red bell peppers.

Avocado Clemson Blue Cheese Dip
Servings: 6

2 medium	Avocados, peeled and pitted	1½ cups	Sour cream
2 Tbsp	Onion, chopped	⅓ cup	Clemson Blue Cheese, crumbled
2 tsp	Lemon juice	¼ tsp	Ground white pepper

In a food processor or blender, purée avocado, onions, and lemon juice until smooth. Add sour cream, Clemson Blue Cheese, and pepper. Purée until well blended and smooth. Place mixture in a serving bowl and refrigerate for 1 to 2 hours before serving. TIP: Serve with bread, crackers, chips, or fresh vegetables.

Clemson Blue Cheese Guacamole
Servings: 16 / Yield: 2¼ cups

2 medium	Avocados	⅓ cup	Clemson Blue Cheese
1 Tbsp	Lemon juice	1 tsp	White pepper
1 Tbsp	Onion, grated	¼ cup	Mayonnaise
½ cup	Tomato, finely chopped		

In a mixing bowl, mash the meat of the avocados. Add lemon juice, grated onion, chopped tomato, Clemson Blue Cheese, and white pepper. Blend until smooth. Place mixture in a bowl, and spread mayonnaise over it to prevent it from browning. Right before serving, blend in the mayonnaise. TIP: Serve with unsalted crackers, chips, or crusty bread.

◀ Shrimp and Clemson Blue Cheese Dip
Servings: 12

12 ounces	Clemson Blue Cheese Dressing II (recipe on pg. 42)	⅓ tsp	Celery seeds
		¼ tsp	Dried thyme
4 ounces	Cooked shrimp, peeled and deveined	¼ tsp	Ground mustard
4	Green onions, finely chopped	¼ tsp	Cayenne pepper powder
1½ cloves	Garlic, minced	2 Tbsp	Clemson Blue Cheese crumbles

In a mixing bowl, combine Clemson Blue Cheese dressing, shrimp, green onions, garlic, celery seeds, thyme, ground mustard, and cayenne pepper. Place mixture in a serving bowl, and sprinkle Clemson Blue Cheese on top. Cover and refrigerate for at least 2 hours. TIP: Serve with fresh vegetables, bread, chips, or crackers.

Clemson Blue Cheese Hummus
Servings: 12

32 ounces	Garbanzo beans, cooked	1½ cup	Clemson Blue Cheese crumbles
½ cup	Tahini	1½ tsp	Garlic mince
¼ cup	Lemon juice	½ tsp	Salt
½ cup	Olive oil	1 tsp	Ground pepper

In a food processor, purée garbanzo beans. Add tahini, lemon juice, olive oil, Clemson Blue Cheese, and garlic. Purée until smooth. Add salt and pepper. Chill before serving. TIP: Serve with toasted pita bread triangles.

Clemson Blue Cheese and Chive Dip
Servings: 12 / Yield: 3 cups

1¼ cups	Sour cream	2 tsp	Lemon juice
1 cup	Clemson Blue Cheese, crumbled	½ bunch	Chives, chopped
¾ cup	Mayonnaise		Salt and pepper
2 Tbsp	Honey		

In a medium mixing bowl, combine sour cream, Clemson Blue Cheese, mayonnaise, and honey. Add lemon juice and chives, and salt and pepper to taste.

Clemson Blue Cheese Spread with Brandy
Servings: 4

2 ounces	Clemson Blue Cheese crumbles
6 ounces	Cream cheese
¼ cup	Brandy

In a food processor or mixing bowl, combine Clemson Blue Cheese and cream cheese and blend well. Add brandy and mix for a smooth, soft consistency. TIP: The brandy can be replaced with cognac, whiskey, rum, or similar liquors.

Clemson Blue Cheese Spread with Pistachios
Servings: 8

8 ounces	Cream cheese	¼ cup	Chopped chives
4 ounces	Clemson Blue Cheese crumbles	1 tsp	Ground white pepper
½ cup	Pistachio nuts, shelled and chopped		

In a medium-size mixing bowl, cream together cream cheese and Clemson Blue Cheese. Add pistachios, chives, and pepper. TIP: Serve with toasted, thinly sliced French bread, Melba toast, or crackers.

Clemson Blue Cheese Spread with Walnuts
Servings: 6

8 ounces	Cream cheese	1 Tbsp	Chives, chopped
4 ounces	Clemson Blue Cheese crumbles	1 Tbsp	Parsley, chopped
¼ cup	Toasted walnuts, finely chopped	1 tsp	Ground white pepper

In a medium-size mixing bowl, combine cream cheese, Clemson Blue Cheese, walnuts, chives, parsley, and pepper. Mix just long enough for ingredients to get incorporated. TIP: Serve with toasted, thinly sliced French bread, Melba toast, or crackers.

Clemson Blue Cheese, Port Wine, and Walnut Spread
Servings: 16 / Yield: 4 cups

1 pound	Clemson Blue Cheese	1½ cups	Toasted walnuts, finely chopped
½ cup	Butter, softened	1 tsp	White pepper
⅓ cup	Port wine		

In a food processor, blend Clemson Blue Cheese, butter, and port wine until smooth. In a bowl, combine the cheese mixture, walnuts, and white pepper. Spoon the mixture into a crock; cover and chill before serving.

Clemson Blue Cheese Artichokes in Spinach Cream Sauce
Servings: 4

6 ounces	Ricotta cheese	2 cups	Bread crumbs
6 ounces	Clemson Blue Cheese	1 cup	Fresh spinach
1 Tbsp	Lemon juice	2 Tbsp	Butter
½ tsp	White pepper	1 Tbsp	Onion, chopped
12 large	Marinated artichoke hearts	1 tsp	Lemon juice
2	Eggs	1 cup	Heavy cream
¾ cup	Buttermilk	1 Tbsp	Parmesan cheese, grated
2 cups	Flour	Salt and pepper	

In a small mixing bowl, combine ricotta cheese, Clemson Blue Cheese, lemon juice, and white pepper; mix well. Spoon the mixture into drained and cored artichokes. Beat together eggs and buttermilk. Roll each artichoke in flour, then in egg mixture, and finally in bread crumbs. Place breaded artichokes on a baking sheet, and bake in a 350-degree oven until well browned (about 15–20 minutes).

FOR THE SAUCE: Remove and discard the stems from the spinach. In a small sauce pan, heat butter over moderate heat. Add onions and sauté until translucent (about 1 minute). Add lemon juice and reduce until almost gone. Add heavy cream and reduce until lightly thickened and smooth. Add spinach and let simmer for 2 minutes. Add salt and pepper to taste. Serve artichokes on a bed of the spinach cream sauce, and sprinkle with Parmesan cheese.

Potato, Bacon, and Clemson Blue Cheese Soufflés
Servings: 8

4 Tbsp	Butter, divided	2 slices	Bacon, cooked and crumbled
2⅔ cups	Mashed potatoes	1 tsp	Salt
⅓ cup	Half and half	½ tsp	Dried thyme leaves
½ cup	Parmesan cheese, grated	½ tsp	Pepper
¼ cup	Clemson Blue Cheese, crumbled	2	Egg whites
2	Egg yolks		

Heat oven to 375F. Butter bottoms and sides of 6 individual (4- to 5-ounce) soufflé dishes or 1 large (5- to 6-cup) soufflé dish. Heat mashed potatoes and remove from heat; stir in cream and 2 tablespoons of butter. Stir in Parmesan cheese, Clemson Blue Cheese, egg yolks, bacon, salt, thyme, and pepper. Using an electric mixer, beat egg whites to soft peaks. Gently fold into potato mixture. Spoon into prepared dishes, filling evenly. Place on middle the oven rack. Bake individual soufflés 30 minutes (40 to 50 minutes for large soufflé) or until soufflés have risen and are lightly browned. Serve immediately.

Fried Clemson Blue Cheese with Strawberry-Ginger Marmalade

Servings: 12

1 pound	Cream cheese	6	Eggs
1 pound	Clemson Blue Cheese	2 cups	Bread crumbs
⅓ cup	Sour cream	1 cup	Strawberry preserves
1	Egg	1 Tbsp	Sherry
½	Onion, diced	1 tsp	Ground ginger
1 Tbsp	Granulated garlic	½ tsp	Curry powder
2 tsp	White pepper	½ tsp	Salt
2 cups	Flour		

In an electric mixing bowl, soften cream cheese with a paddle. Add Clemson Blue Cheese, sour cream, egg, onion, garlic, and pepper. Mix until all ingredients are combined and smooth. Divide mixture into 12 portions and shape into ½-inch patties. Place patties on a sheet pan with parchment paper, cover, and freeze. Bread Clemson Blue Cheese patties by dredging them first in flour, then in egg-wash (whipped whole eggs), and finally in bread crumbs. Repeat procedure. Deep-fry at 350F for 2 to 3 minutes until golden brown.

STRAWBERRY-GINGER MARMALADE: In a small mixing bowl, combine strawberry preserves, sherry, ginger, curry, and salt. Mix well. TIP: Serve with toasted pita points and garnish with mixed lettuce.

Clemson Blue Cheese Torta

Servings: 8

8 ounces	Clemson Blue Cheese, crumbled	½ tsp	White pepper
12 ounces	Cream cheese	¾ cup	Sun-dried tomato pesto
1 tsp	Granulated garlic		

In a mixing bowl or food processor, combine Clemson Blue Cheese, cream cheese, granulated garlic, and pepper. Mix until smooth. Line a small bowl with plastic wrap, allowing a few inches to hang over the sides. Spread ⅓ of cheese mixture into the bowl; top with ½ of the sun-dried tomato pesto; top with another ⅓ of cheese mixture, and top that with the remaining sun-dried tomato pesto. Finish with remaining cheese mixture. Cover and chill for at least 4 hours. Invert torta onto a serving platter; remove plastic wrap. TIP: Serve with baguette, melba toast, or crackers.

Escargot with Clemson Blue Cheese
Servings: 1

For each person, sauté half- chopped shallot in 1 teaspoon of olive oil; add 1 teaspoon of roasted garlic, 1 chopped mushroom, and 2 teaspoons of chopped tomatoes. Add 6 escargots, 2 teaspoons of port wine, and 1 tablespoon of heavy cream. Reduce until lightly thickened. Add 1 tablespoon of Clemson Blue Cheese crumbles, and salt and pepper to taste. Serve in a small bowl or ramekin with baguette or toasted bread.

Clemson Blue Cheese and Spiced Nut Terrine

Servings: 24

2 Tbsp	Butter	1 pound	Clemson Blue Cheese, crumbled
1 tsp	Cumin	6 ounces	Boursin cheese
1 tsp	Allspice	2 Tbsp	Butter
¼ tsp	Cayenne	½ cup	Green onion, chopped
8 ounces	Mixed nuts	¼ cup	Brandy
2 Tbsp	Sugar	2 Tbsp	Parsley, chopped
1 tsp	Salt	1 Tbsp	Chives, chopped

In an ovenproof sauté pan or skillet, melt butter and add cumin, allspice, and cayenne. Pour in nuts, sugar, and salt, and stir to coat. Place pan or skillet in a 300-degree oven for 20 minutes. Remove from oven and allow it to cool before coarsely chopping the nuts. Lightly oil a loaf pan (8½ x 2½). Line pan with plastic wrap so that plastic extends over edges. In a mixing bowl or food processor, combine Clemson Blue Cheese, Boursin cheese, and butter, and blend until smooth. Stir in green onions, brandy, parsley, and chives.

Spread ⅓ of the cheese mixture evenly into the bottom of the lined pan. Sprinkle ½ of the nuts over evenly. Spoon another ⅓ of the cheese mixture over the nuts, and sprinkle another layer of nuts over that. Top with the last ⅓ of the cheese mixture. Fold plastic over cheese to cover. Refrigerate 3 to 4 hours (or overnight). Unfold plastic from top of cheese, and carefully invert mold onto platter; remove loaf pan and plastic.

Cashew and Clemson Blue Cheese Crostini with Cranberries

Servings: 8

1½ cups	Cashews	1 cup	Dried cranberries
8 ounces	Clemson Blue Cheese, crumbled	1 loaf	Baguette

In a food processor, chop cashews and cranberries. Add Clemson Blue Cheese and blend until just combined. Cut baguette into ¼-inch slices. Place slices on a baking sheet and bake in a 400-degree oven for a few minutes until lightly brown. Place a large dollop of Clemson Blue Cheese mixture on each slice, and return to the oven for 1 to 2 minutes to lightly melt cheese.

Clemson Blue Cheese Cucumber Rounds

Yield: 32 / Servings: 8

2 ounces	Cream cheese	3 medium	Radishes
2 ounces	Clemson Blue Cheese	16	Chives
½ medium	Seedless cucumber		

In a small bowl, stir together cream cheese, and Clemson Blue Cheese. Slice 32 (⅛-inch thick) rounds from cucumber. Trim bottoms from radishes, and slice into 32 (1/16-inch thick) rounds. Top each cucumber slice with a radish slice and ½ teaspoon of cheese mixture. Cut each chive into 4, and place 2 on each cheese round.

Clemson Blue Cheese and Pistachio Stuffed Strawberries ▶
Servings: 8

16 large	Strawberries	½ tsp	Ground white pepper
4 ounces	Cream cheese	2 Tbsp	Balsamic vinegar
2 ounces	Clemson Blue Cheese crumbles	2 Tbsp	Olive oil
¼ cup	Pistachios, shelled and chopped	Salt and pepper	
2 Tbsp	Chives, chopped		

Cut a sliver of each strawberry and reserve. Using a small melon baller, hollow out a small portion of the strawberry and set aside. In a medium-size mixing bowl, mix together cream cheese and Clemson Blue Cheese. Add pistachios, chives, and pepper, and mix to combine. Pipe cheese mixture into the strawberries. Cut each of the reserve strawberry slivers into 3 pieces lengthwise, the middle one being the smallest. Place the middle one on the top end of the Clemson Blue Cheese filling as a "head," and place the remaining pieces on the sides as "wings."

In a blender, purée the reserved hollowed-out strawberries and balsamic vinegar. Slowly pour in the olive oil. Add salt and pepper to taste. Pour thin strips of vinegar mixture onto plates, and place strawberries on top.

Clemson Blue Cheese and Pecan-Crusted Tomato Slices
Servings: 10

5 large	Tomatoes	2 Tbsp	Parsley, finely minced
⅔ cup	Clemson Blue Cheese, crumbled	1 cup	Pecans, finely chopped
⅔ cup	Cream cheese, softened	Ground white pepper to taste	

Core tomatoes and remove enough pulp to make a narrow opening for the cheese stuffing. Turn tomatoes upside down to drain seeds and juices. In a mixing bowl, combine Clemson Blue Cheese, cream cheese, parsley, and pepper. Stuff each tomato with the cheese mixture, packing it firmly. Refrigerate stuffed tomatoes for at least 1 hour. When ready to serve, cut into thick slices. Sprinkle pecans over tomato slices, leaving cheese visible. Use 2 to 3 slices per portion.

Clemson Blue Cheese Bruschetta
Yield: 12 / Servings: 4

2 ounces	Clemson Blue Cheese, crumbled	⅛ tsp	Ground white pepper
2 ounces	Butter, softened	12 slices	French baguette, 1-inch thick
1 Tbsp	Brandy	Cooking spray	
¼ tsp	Granulated garlic		

In a small mixing bowl, combine Clemson Blue Cheese, butter, brandy, garlic, and white pepper. Spray bread slices with cooking spray, and bake in 375-degree oven for 2 minutes or until lightly browned. Spread cheese mixture over each bread slice. TIP: Serve with grapes, apple, or pear wedges.

Broccoli Clemson Blue Cheese Soup
Servings: 8

2 ounces	Butter	1½ cups	Whole milk
1	Onion, chopped	1 cup	Clemson Blue Cheese, crumbled
1	Broccoli head, chopped	½ cup	Heavy cream
6 Tbsp	Flour	1 cup	Croutons
3½ cups	Chicken stock		Salt and pepper

Melt butter in a medium-size sauce pan, add onion, and sauté for about 3 minutes without browning. Stir in flour and cook for 1 minute. Add broccoli and stock. Bring to a boil, stirring continuously until soup thickens. Simmer on low heat for 15 minutes. Purée soup in food processor or blender. Return to saucepan and heat gently. Stir in Clemson Blue Cheese and heavy cream, and heat until cheese is melted. Do not allow soup to boil at this point. Add salt and pepper to taste. Ladle soup into soup bowls, and garnish with croutons.

Cauliflower, Potato, and Leek Cream Soup with Clemson Blue Cheese Butter
Servings: 10

1 pound	Cauliflower, chopped	4 ounces	Clemson Blue Cheese and cracked peppercorn butter, sliced (pg. 45)
1 pound	Potatoes, peeled and chopped		
2	Leeks, diced and rinsed		
4 cups	Water		Salt and pepper
1 cup	Sour cream		

Place cauliflower, potatoes, and leeks in a large soup pot with the water and simmer until done, about 30 minutes. Remove half of the cauliflower, potatoes, and leeks, and save. In a blender or food processor, purée the remaining half plus all the liquid with the sour cream. Return the soup to the pot, and add the saved vegetables. Reheat the soup if necessary. Add salt and pepper to taste. Serve in a bowl or soup cups topped with a thin slice of Clemson Blue Cheese butter on top.

Sweet Potato and Clemson Blue Cheese Soup
Servings: 6

2 pounds	Sweet potatoes, peeled and cubed	2 Tbsp	Lemon juice
6 cups	Chicken stock or chicken broth	2 Tbsp	Heavy cream
5 ounces	Clemson Blue Cheese, crumbled		Salt and pepper

In a large soup pot, simmer sweet potatoes in chicken stock until done (about 15 minutes). Purée sweet potatoes and stock in a food processor and return to soup pot. Add lemon juice and 4 ounces of Clemson Blue Cheese crumbles. Heat slowly without boiling until cheese is melted. Add salt and pepper to taste, and ladle soup into soup cups or bowls. Drizzle heavy cream over the soup and sprinkle with remaining 1 ounce Clemson Blue Cheese.

French Onion Soup with Clemson Blue Cheese Croutons

For 4 servings, cut off the top and bottom of 2 large onions. Remove the skin, cut each onion in half, and thinly slice them into half circles. In a medium-size sauce pot, heat a combination of olive oil and butter (about 2 tablespoons of each). Add the sliced onions and cook, occasionally stirring, for 20 to 30 minutes until onions are soft and dark brown. Add 1 tablespoon of chopped garlic and 1 teaspoon of dried thyme leaves. Pour in 3 cups of stock or broth (chicken, beef, or vegetable stock, or in any combination). Scraping the bottom of the pot, bring soup to a boil and simmer for 10 to 12 minutes, Adjust the flavor with salt and pepper. (½ cup of dry red wine or sherry vastly improves the flavor.)

Cut 8 ½-inch slices of a French baguette. Top each slice with 2 teaspoons Clemson Blue Cheese crumbles and bake in a 400-degree oven until cheese is hot and slightly melted. Ladle the hot soup into soup cups or soup crocks, and place 2 croutons on top of each. Serve immediately.

Pumpkin Soup with Clemson Blue Cheese and Bacon

Servings: 6

2 ounces	Butter		1 tsp	Nutmeg
1	Onion, chopped		1 tsp	Salt
2 pound	Cooked pumpkin		¼ tsp	Cayenne
1 quart	Chicken stock		6 slices	Bacon
1 cup	Half and half		1 cup	Clemson Blue Cheese, crumbled
½ cup	Honey			

Melt butter in a medium-size saucepan; add onion, and sauté (about 3 minutes). Add pumpkin, chicken stock, half and half, honey, nutmeg, salt, and cayenne; bring to a boil and simmer for 10 minutes, stirring occasionally.

Cook bacon in a large skillet until crispy; transfer to a dish with a paper towel to drain. Ladle soup into bowls and top with Clemson Blue Cheese. Crumble bacon and sprinkle over the blue cheese.

Chilled Tomato and Clemson Blue Cheese Soup
Servings: 8

5 cups	Tomato juice	2 Tbsp	Honey
3 ounces	Cream cheese, softened	1 tsp	Lemon juice
1 small	Onion, chopped	½ tsp	White pepper
2 Tbsp	Fresh basil, chopped	4 ounces	Clemson Blue Cheese, crumbled
1 Tbsp	Soy sauce		

In a blender or food processor, combine, 1 cup of the tomato juice with cream cheese, onion, basil, honey, lemon juice, pepper, and half of the Clemson Blue Cheese. Process slowly, adding the remaining tomato juice. Pour soup into a large bowl and chill. To serve, ladle soup into bowls, and sprinkle remaining Clemson Blue Cheese on top.

Spinach and Clemson Blue Cheese Soup with Coconut
Servings: 16

4 ounces	Butter	24 ounces	Spinach, chopped
2 cups	Onion, chopped	1 cup	Heavy cream
1 cup	Flour	8 ounces	Clemson Blue Cheese, crumbled
3 quarts	Chicken stock	1 tsp	Cayenne
4 cups	Milk	½ cup	Coconut, shredded

In a large pot over medium heat, melt butter and add onions. Sauté for about 3 minutes. Add flour and stir until well mixed. Add chicken stock and milk; bring to a boil, and simmer (about 10 minutes). Whisk mixture to keep flour from clumping. Add spinach and cook 3 more minutes. Add the heavy cream, Clemson Blue Cheese, and cayenne and heat to almost a boil. Turn off heat and stir well. Sprinkle shredded coconut onto a baking pan and bake in a 350-degree oven for about 2 minutes or until golden brown. Purée soup in a food processor or blender. Ladle into individual bowls, and sprinkle with toasted coconut.

Clemson Clam Chowder
Servings: 8

4 ounces	Bacon, diced	14 fl. ounces	Clam juice
2 ounces	Butter	4 ounces	Potatoes, peeled and diced
2 ounces	Onion, chopped	1 cup	Half and half
2 ounces	Celery, chopped	¼ tsp	Dried thyme
2 ounces	Flour	¼ tsp	White pepper
14 ounces	Canned chopped clams, drained (save juices)	1 tsp	Salt
		½ cup	Clemson Blue Cheese crumbles

In a heavy sauce pot, sauté bacon in butter. Add onions and celery, and sauté until soft (about 3 to 4 minutes). Add flour and incorporate without browning. Add clam juices and potatoes; simmer for about 20 minutes. Add half and half and return to a simmer; add clams, spices, salt, and half of the Clemson Blue Cheese. Pour into cups and sprinkle remaining Clemson Blue Cheese on top.

Arugula Salad with Clemson Blue Cheese, Bacon, and Hazelnuts
Servings: 4

3 Tbsp	Vegetable oil	½ tsp	Ground black pepper
5 slices	Thick-sliced bacon, cut crosswise into ½-inch pieces	4 ounces	Clemson Blue Cheese crumbles
		3 cups	Arugula leaves
4 Tbsp	Red wine vinegar	3 Tbsp	Hazelnuts, chopped and toasted

Place oil in a large sauté pan over medium-high heat. Add bacon and sauté until brown and crisp. Carefully pour bacon and fat into a large bowl. Add vinegar, pepper, and Clemson Blue Cheese. Stir to incorporate. Add arugula and toss to combine. Divide the salad onto plates, and sprinkle with hazelnuts.

Clemson Blue Cheese Salad with Grapefruit and Avocado
Servings: 6

4 cups	Bibb lettuce, torn	3 Tbsp	Clemson Blue Cheese crumbles
2 cups	Arugula	½ cup	Grapefruit juice
1¼ cups	Grapefruit sectio	¼ cup	Italian dressing
1	Avocado, peeled and chopped	3 Tbsp	Vegetable oil

Divide Bibb lettuce and arugula on 6 salad plates; arrange grapefruit sections and avocado over the lettuce, and sprinkle with Clemson Blue Cheese crumbles. In a small mixing bowl, combine grapefruit juice and Italian dressing, and whisk in vegetable oil. Pour dressing over the salads, or serve it on the side.

Clemson Blue Cheese Mushroom Salad
Servings: 8

20 ounces	Mushrooms, sliced (about 6 cups)	1 cup	Corn kernels, cooked
		½ cup	Pimento, diced
2 cups	Basil vinaigrette (see pg. 42)	1	Radicchio lettuce
8 ounces	Snow peas, cut diagonally in ¼ strips (about 3 cups)	2	Belgian endive
		1	Romaine lettuce
1 cup	Watercress, coarsely chopped	4 ounces	Clemson Blue Cheese, crumbled
1 cup	Red onion, diced		

In a large bowl, marinate mushrooms in basil vinaigrette for 30 minutes. Add snow peas, watercress, red onion, corn, and pimentos; toss gently. For each serving, make a cup using radicchio, endive, and romaine lettuce leaves. Fill cup with mushroom-vegetable mixture. Top with Clemson Blue Cheese.

Baked Sweet Potato and Clemson Blue Cheese Salad
with Dijon Vinaigrette
Servings: 4

1 medium	Sweet potato, peeled and cubed	2 tsp	Honey
1 Tbsp	Vegetable oil	1 Tbsp	Worcestershire sauce
2 cups	Mixed salad greens	½ tsp	Salt
1 cup	Watercress, stems removed	½ tsp	Ground white pepper
2 Tbsp	Lemon juice	3 Tbsp	Olive oil
1 Tbsp	Dijon mustard	3 ounces	Clemson Blue Cheese crumbles

In a small bowl, toss sweet potatoes with vegetable oil. Spread onto a baking dish and bake in 375-degree oven until done but still firm (about 20 minutes). Remove from oven and chill. In a large bowl, combine salad greens and watercress.

In a small jar with a tight fitting lid, combine lemon juice, mustard, honey, Worcestershire sauce, salt, pepper, and olive oil. Shake jar, pour vinaigrette over salad greens, and toss gently. Arrange greens on salad plates, and top with sweet potatoes. Sprinkle with Clemson Blue Cheese.

Napa Clemson Blue Cheese Coleslaw
Servings: 16

2 pounds	Napa cabbage, shredded	1 Tbsp	Sugar
10 ounces	Clemson Blue Cheese, crumbled	1 tsp	Salt
⅓ cup	Onion, chopped	1 tsp	White pepper
2 cloves	Garlic, chopped	⅓ cup	White vinegar
2 tsp	Celery Seed	¾ cup	Vegetable oil
½ tsp	Dry mustard		

In a large bowl, combine cabbage and Clemson Blue Cheese. In a medium mixing bowl, whisk together onion, garlic, celery seeds, dry mustard, sugar, salt, pepper, and vinegar. Add oil in a thin stream while whisking to emulsify. Pour dressing over cabbage before tossing.

Belgian Endive Leaves with Clemson Blue Cheese and Walnuts
Yield: 30 leaves / Servings: 10

6 ounces	Clemson Blue Cheese, room temperature	1 Tbsp	Fresh parsley, minced
		pinch	Fresh-ground black pepper
2 Tbsp	Heavy cream	2 heads	Belgian endive, leaves separated
¼ cup	Walnuts, chopped		

In a medium bowl, combine the cheese, cream, walnuts, parsley, and pepper. Mix with a wooden spoon until smooth and creamy. Place 1½ tsps of the cheese mixture onto each endive leaf. Arrange on platter.

Oven-Roasted Pears with Clemson Blue Cheese Salad ▶

Servings: 6

4 ounces	Clemson Blue Cheese, crumbled	¼ cup	Port wine
¼ cup	Dried cranberries	⅓ cup	Honey
¼ cup	Toasted pecans, chopped	¼ cup	Olive oil
3	Pears, ripe but firm	6 ounces	Mixed baby lettuce
½ cup	Apple juice	Salt and pepper	

In a small mixing bowl, combine Clemson Blue Cheese, cranberries, and pecans. Peel pears and cut them in halves lengthwise. Using a melon baller, remove core and seeds from each pear. Arrange them core side up in a small baking dish. Divide the cheese mixture among the pears.

In the same small bowl, combine apple juice, port wine, and honey. Pour ½ of the mixture over the pears, and bake at 350F oven until pears are tender (about 30 minutes).

Just before serving, whisk olive oil into the port wine mixture; and add salt and pepper to taste. Arrange baby lettuce among 6 plates, and top each with a warm pear. Drizzle dressing over salad and serve.

Mixed Lettuce with Avocado, Pear, and Clemson Blue Cheese

Servings: 12

¼ cup	White vinegar	10 cups	Mixed salad greens
1 tsp	Dijon mustard	2	Pears, ripe and thinly sliced
½ tsp	Salt	2	Oranges, sectioned
1 tsp	Dried basil	2	Avocados, sliced
⅓ cup	Olive oil	4 ounces	Clemson Blue Cheese, crumbled

For the dressing, mix vinegar, mustard, salt, and basil, and whisk in olive oil.
Put mixed greens in a large serving bowl, and arrange pears, oranges, avocados, and Clemson Blue Cheese on top. Drizzle dressing and serve.

Clemson Blue Cheese Potato Salad

Servings: 12

5 pounds	New potatoes	8 ounces	Clemson Blue Cheese, crumbled
½ cup	White wine	4 strips	Bacon, cooked and crumbled
3 Tbsp	White vinegar	Ground white pepper	
2 Tbsp	Honey		

Boil potatoes in a large pot of lightly salted water until tender. Drain, cool slightly, and peel potatoes. Cut into 1-inch pieces. In a large bowl, combine wine, pepper, vinegar, honey, and Clemson Blue Cheese. Add potatoes and toss well. Adjust seasoning and sprinkle bacon on top.

◀ Endive Salad with Clemson Blue Cheese
Servings: 2

2 small	Endives		1 Tbsp	Cottage cheese
1 small	Pear, thinly sliced		1 clove	Garlic, crushed
½ cup	Watercress		1 tsp	Lemon juice
½ cup	Walnut halves		3 tsp	Walnut oil
¼ cup	Clemson Blue Cheese			Salt and pepper

Cut bottom of the endives, and separate the leaves. Rinse the endive leaves and watercress. Arrange the endive leaves in a circle on chilled plates and the pear slices over the endive. Arrange the watercress in the middle, and sprinkle walnuts and Clemson Blue Cheese on top. Place cottage cheese and garlic in a mixing bowl or food processor, and blend in the lemon juice and the oil in a thin stream. Add salt and pepper to taste. Pour dressing over the salads and serve.

Curly Endive, Bacon, and Clemson Blue Cheese Salad
Servings: 4

4 ounces	Bacon, cut in cubes		2 Tbsp	Clemson Blue Cheese vinaigrette
4 ounces	Curly endive			Salt and Pepper
4 ounces	Clemson Blue Cheese, crumbled			

Cook bacon in a skillet, stirring frequently until it browns and crisps. Place curly endive in a large salad bowl. Using a slotted spoon, transfer the bacon to the salad bowl, add Clemson Blue Cheese and Clemson Blue Cheese vinaigrette; toss to mix. Add salt and pepper, toss again, and serve.

Green Salad with Clemson Blue Cheese
Servings: 4

2 Tbsp	Vinegar		¼ cup	Red onions, chopped
⅓ cup	Salad oil		2	Hard boiled eggs, chopped
¼ cup	Clemson Blue Cheese, crumbled		4 cups	Mixed green lettuce, bite-size pieces
1 tsp	Paprika			
½ tsp	Worcestershire sauce		8	Cherry tomato, halved
1	Avocado			Salt and pepper
1 Tbsp	Lemon juice			

In a small mixing bowl, mix vinegar, oil, Clemson Blue Cheese, paprika, Worcestershire sauce, salt, and pepper. Chill. Peel and chop the avocado, and sprinkle with lemon juice. Combine avocado, onions, eggs, and lettuce in a bowl. Pour dressing over mixture and toss well. Place salad on plates, and garnish with cherry tomatoes.

Rice Salad with Pecans and Clemson Blue Cheese

Servings: 12

3 cups	Cooked rice, hot	1 cup	Sour cream
¼ cup	Onion, finely chopped	⅓ cup	Clemson Blue Cheese, crumbled
1 cup	Celery, finely chopped	1 Tbsp	Rice vinegar
¼ cup	Pimentos, chopped	1 Tbsp	Salt
3	Hard boiled eggs, chopped	½ Tbsp	Ground white pepper
⅓ cup	Pecans, chopped		

In a mixing bowl, combine rice, onions, celery, pimentos, eggs, and pecans. Add sour cream, Clemson Blue Cheese, rice vinegar, salt, and pepper. Spoon rice mixture into a mold, and chill thoroughly. Unmold before serving.

Orzo Clemson Blue Cheese Salad

Servings: 6

1 cup	Orzo pasta	3 Tbsp	Balsamic vinegar
3 cups	Baby spinach	¼ cup	Walnuts, toasted
6 strips	Bacon, cooked and chopped	1 clove	Garlic
3 ounces	Clemson Blue Cheese, crumbled	1 tsp	Dijon mustard
¼ cup	Walnuts, toasted and chopped	⅓ cup	Salad oil
¼ cup	Green onion, chopped		

Cook orzo in lightly salted water; drain. In a mixing bowl, combine orzo, baby spinach, bacon, Clemson Blue Cheese, walnuts, and green onions. In a blender or food processor, combine vinegar, walnuts, garlic, and Dijon mustard; cover and process until smooth. Gradually add oil in a thin stream. Pour dressing over salad; toss and serve.

Watercress-Orange Salad with Clemson Blue Cheese

Servings: 4

1 bunch	Watercress	¼ tsp	Dried tarragon
2	Oranges, peeled and sectioned	¼ cup	Vegetable oil
½ small	Red onion, thinly sliced	4 ounces	Clemson Blue Cheese crumbles
2 Tbsp	White vinegar	Salt and pepper	
1 tsp	Dijon mustard		

Wash watercress and discard large stems. Place watercress, orange sections, and onions in a large bowl. In a small mixing bowl, combine vinegar, Dijon mustard, and tarragon. Whisk in oil and add salt and pepper to taste. Drizzle dressing over watercress mixture, and toss to coat. Sprinkle Clemson Blue Cheese over the salad.

Watermelon and Clemson Blue Cheese Salad
with Toasted Sunflower Seeds

Cut the rind of a seedless watermelon (a mix of red and yellow watermelon works well). Cut watermelon into bite-size pieces, and place in a large bowl. Add toasted sunflower seeds, Clemson Blue Cheese crumbles, and thinly sliced red onion, arugula, or mixed baby lettuce. Mix well.

Place salad in individual bowls; pour your favorite vinaigrette and serve.

◀ Clemson Blue Cheese Waldorf Salad
Servings: 4

2 medium	Apples, cored and diced	½ cup	Mayonnaise
2 Tbsp	Lemon juice	½ cup	Walnuts, roughly chopped
1 cup	Dried cranberries	2 Tbsp	Clemson Blue Cheese crumbles
1 cup	Celery, sliced		

In a medium serving bowl, toss apples in lemon juice. Add cranberries, celery, mayonnaise, walnuts, and Clemson Blue Cheese; mix well. Chill before serving.

Western Waldorf Salad
Servings: 4

2 large	Apples, cored and diced	1 tsp	Dijon-style mustard
1 Tbsp	Lemon juice	½ tsp	Salt
½ cup	Seedless red grapes, halved	¼ tsp	Ground black pepper
2 Tbsp	Walnut oil	4 Tbsp	Walnuts, chopped and toasted
2 Tbsp	Cider vinegar	3 Tbsp	Clemson Blue Cheese crumbles

In a medium bowl, toss diced apples with lemon juice; toss in grape halves. In a small bowl, stir together oil, vinegar, mustard, salt, and pepper; pour over apple mixture, and toss well. Portion onto 4 salad plates; top each salad with walnuts and Clemson Blue Cheese.

Tomato and Avocado Salad with Clemson Blue Cheese
Servings: 2

2 ounces	Clemson Blue Cheese, crumbled	1 head	Romaine lettuce, broken into bite-size pieces
2 Tbsp	Red wine vinegar		
4 Tbsp	Olive oil	2	Green onions, chopped
1	Tomato, chopped	1	Avocado, chopped

In a small mixing bowl, combine Clemson Blue Cheese, vinegar, and olive oil. In a salad bowl, combine lettuce, tomato, green onions, and avocado. Pour vinaigrette and toss.

Clemson Blue Cheese Coleslaw
Servings: 16

3 Tbsp	Sugar	12 ounces	Clemson Blue Cheese, crumbled
3 Tbsp	White vinegar	8 cups	Cabbage, shredded
16 ounces	Sour cream		

In a large mixing bowl, combine sugar and vinegar. Add and blend sour cream and Clemson Blue Cheese. Pour mixture over shredded cabbage, and mix thoroughly. Refrigerate at least 2 hours before serving.

Roasted Sweet Potato, Clemson Blue Cheese, and Arugula Salad
Servings: 4

1½ pound	Sweet potatoes, peeled and cubed	1 cup	Arugula leaves
2 Tbsp	Vegetable oil	½ cup	Clemson Blue Cheese vinaigrette
2 cups	Iceberg lettuce, chopped	¼ cup	Clemson Blue Cheese, crumbled

Place sweet potatoes in a baking dish, and sprinkle with oil. Roast in 375-degree oven for 20 minutes or until tender but firm; cool. In a large mixing bowl, combine iceberg and arugula. Add about ½ the vinaigrette, and toss gently to coat the leaves. Arrange lettuce on serving plates, and top with sweet potatoes; sprinkle with Clemson Blue Cheese, and drizzle with remaining vinaigrette.

Rotini Salad with Clemson Blue Cheese and Bacon
Servings: 4

4 ounces	Bacon, sliced	1 Tbsp	Parsley, chopped
2 Tbsp	White vinegar	8 ounces	Dried rotini pasta, cooked
1 clove	Garlic, minced	1 cup	Celery, thinly sliced
½ tsp	Ground white pepper	3 ounces	Clemson Blue Cheese, crumbled
¼ cup	Olive oil		

Cook bacon in the oven or in a skillet until crisp. Drain and chop. In a large mixing bowl, whisk together vinegar, garlic, pepper, olive oil, and chopped parsley. Add pasta and mix well. Sprinkle with bacon and Clemson Blue Cheese, and mix lightly. Arrange pasta salad on a serving platter or on individual salad plates.

Mixed Greens with Baked Clemson Blue Cheese Stuffed Figs
Servings: 6

6 cups	Mixed baby greens	1 Tbsp	Madeira
9	Black mission figs	1 Tbsp	Balsamic vinegar
⅓ cup	Clemson Blue Cheese, crumbles	3 Tbsp	Vegetable oil
3 Tbsp	Olive oil	Fresh ground pepper	
2 Tbsp	Toasted hazelnuts	Salt and pepper	
1 Tbsp	Shallots, chopped		

Arrange baby greens on salad plates. Cut figs in half and place them on a baking sheet cut side up. Divide Clemson Blue Cheese on top and sprinkle with olive oil and fresh pepper. Bake in a 400-degree oven until cheese starts to melt (about 2 to 3 minutes). Arrange 3 halves of warm figs on each plate. Combine hazelnuts, shallots, Madeira, and balsamic vinegar. When ready to serve, whisk in vegetable oil. Add salt and pepper to taste, and sprinkle over salad.

TASTES OF CLEMSON BLUE CHEESE
Dressing & Sauces

Basil Vinaigrette
Servings: 10 / Yield: 1¼ cups

⅓ cup	Fresh basil, chopped		¾ cup	Vegetable oil
2 Tbsp	Dijon mustard		⅓ cup	White wine vinegar
1½ tsp	Salt		1 Tbsp	Fresh lemon juice
¾ tsp	Ground black pepper			

In a small bowl, combine basil, mustard, salt, pepper, oil, vinegar, and lemon juice. Stir just before using. (Use when preparing Clemson Blue Cheese and Mushroom Salad on pg. 30)

Clemson Blue Cheese Dressing
Servings: 32 / Yield: 1 quart

1 cup	Mayonnaise		1 tsp	Worcestershire sauce
2 tsp	Red wine vinegar		½ tsp	Tabasco sauce
1 cup	Sour cream		¼ tsp	Pepper
½ cup	Buttermilk		1½ cups	Clemson Blue Cheese, crumbled
1 tsp	Garlic, chopped			

Combine all the ingredients except the Clemson Blue Cheese; mix well. Add the crumbled Clemson Blue Cheese and combine.

Clemson Blue Cheese Dressing I
Servings: 8

3 ounces	Clemson Blue Cheese		¼ cup	Yogurt
1½ Tbsp	Sherry vinegar		1 tsp	Chopped chives
¼ cup	Olive oil		½ tsp	White pepper

Place Clemson Blue Cheese crumbles in a bowl, and whisk in vinegar and then oil. Add yogurt, blend well, and add chives and pepper.

Clemson Blue Cheese Dressing II
Servings: 8

½ cups	Mayonnaise		pinch	White pepper
2 Tbsp	Heavy cream		2 Tbsp	Clemson Blue Cheese, crumbled
⅓ cup	Sour cream		½ tsp	Parsley, chopped
⅓ tsp	Garlic, chopped			

Combine all ingredients in a mixing bowl.

Clemson Blue Cheese Dressing III
Servings: 24

4 ounces   Clemson Blue Cheese, crumbled
1½ cups   Mayonnaise
1 cup   Heavy cream, whipped

In a mixing bowl, beat Clemson Blue Cheese and mayonnaise until smooth. Fold in the whipped cream, and chill until ready to use.

Clemson Blue Cheese Dressing IV
Servings: 8

½ cup   Buttermilk   3 ounce   Clemson Blue Cheese, crumbled
¼ cup   Vegetable oil   ¼ tsp   Ground white pepper
2 Tbsp Chives, chopped

In a blender or food processor, blend buttermilk, oil, chives, pepper, and half the Clemson Blue Cheese until smooth; stir in remaining Clemson Blue Cheese.

Low-Fat Clemson Blue Cheese Dressing
Servings: 8 / Yield: 1 quart

6 ounces	Nonfat yogurt	¼ tsp	Worcestershire sauce
2 ounces	Low-fat buttermilk	¼ tsp	Dry mustard
1 ounces	Clemson Blue Cheese, crumbled	¼ tsp	Tabasco sauce
¼ tsp	White pepper		

In a bowl, mixer or food processor, combine all ingredients and process until smooth.

Clemson Blue Cheese Dressing with Brandy
Servings: 8 / Yield: 2 cups

1 cup	Sour cream	2 tsp	Onion, chopped
¾ cup	Mayonnaise	2 Tbsp	Brandy
4 ounces	Clemson Blue Cheese, crumbled	1 tsp	Celery seed
1 clove	Garlic, finely chopped	½ tsp	Ground white pepper

In a mixing bowl, combine sour cream, mayonnaise, and Clemson Blue Cheese. Add garlic, onion, brandy, celery seeds, and pepper. Mix thoroughly.

Clemson Blue Cheese Vinaigrette
Servings: 6

¼ cup	Clemson Blue Cheese, crumbled	pinch	White pepper
¼ tsp	Garlic, granulated	6 Tbsp	Olive oil
2 Tbsp	White wine vinegar		

In a mixing bowl, combine the Clemson Blue Cheese, garlic, vinegar, and pepper. Add the olive oil in a slow steady stream, whisking constantly to incorporate.

Clemson Blue Cheese Vinaigrette II
Servings: 6

4 ounces	Clemson Blue Cheese, crumbled	½ cup	Walnut oil
3 Tbsp	Lemon juice	½ tsp	Ground white pepper

Place all ingredients in a jar with a tight-fitting lid. Right before serving, shake jar to incorporate all ingredients.

Clemson Blue Cheese and Cracked Peppercorn Butter
Servings: 12

10 ounces	Unsalted butter, softened
3 ounces	Clemson Blue Cheese, crumbled
1 ounce	Black pepper, cracked

Combine butter, Clemson Blue Cheese, and pepper in a mixing bowl, and blend thoroughly. Roll in plastic wrap and refrigerate.

Clemson Blue Cheese Cream Sauce
Servings: 8

4 Tbsp	Butter	6 ounces	Clemson Blue Cheese crumbles
2	Shallots, finely chopped	¼ tsp	Ground white pepper
½ cup	Heavy cream		

In a small sauce pan, heat butter. Add shallots and cook for 3 to 4 minutes or until soft, but not brown. Add heavy cream and bring to a boil. Remove sauce pan from heat, and stir in Clemson Blue Cheese crumbles; add pepper.

Clemson Blue Cheese Mornay
Servings: 16 / Yield: 1 quart

2 ounces	Butter	2 ounces	Flour
1 quart	Milk		Salt and white pepper
4 ounces	Clemson Blue Cheese, crumbled		Nutmeg

In a medium saucepan, melt butter and add flour. Stir over medium heat for about 2 minutes without browning. Whisk in milk and bring it to a simmer while whisking. Reduce heat, and simmer gently (about 20 minutes). Strain sauce and add Clemson Blue Cheese, salt, pepper, and a little nutmeg.

Clemson Blue Cheese and Brandy Mayonnaise
Servings: 8 / Yield: 1 cup

2 ounces	Clemson Blue Cheese, crumbled	1 Tbsp	Brandy
3 ounces	Cream cheese	1 Tbsp	White wine
¼ cup	Mayonnaise	pinch	White pepper

In a mixing bowl, combine all ingredients, and mix until creamy.

Clemsonnaise Sauce
Servings: 8 / Yield: 2 cups

1 cup	Clarified butter	2 Tbsp	White wine
	(about 10 ounces before clarifying)	Dashes	Cayenne pepper
4	Egg yolks	¼ cup	Clemson Blue Cheese, crumbled
1 Tbsp	Lemon juice		

In a small sauce pan, heat an inch of water over medium heat. In a small stainless steel bowl, combine egg yolks, lemon juice, and white wine. Set the bowl directly atop the saucepan of simmering water. The water should not touch the bottom of the bowl. Whisk egg mixture until it is slightly thickened; this will take several minutes. Turn off the heat and slowly add the warm (but not hot) clarified butter, whisking constantly. Start with a few drops at a time, and as the sauce thickens, gradually increase the amount. If it gets too thick, add a few drops of white wine or water. Add cayenne pepper and Clemson Blue Cheese. Whisk until cheese is melted and the sauce is smooth. Serve with poached eggs, chicken, steak, asparagus, broccoli, or cauliflower.

Clemson Blue Cheese Mustard
Servings: 16 / Yield: 2 ½ cups

2 Tbsp	Olive oil		12 ounces	Dark beer
1 Tbsp	Garlic, chopped		4 ounces	Clemson Blue Cheese crumbles
1 Tbsp	Cracked black pepper		1 cup	Dijon-style mustard
1 Tbsp	Lemon juice			

Heat oil in a heavy sauce pan, and add garlic. Cook for 1 minute and add pepper, lemon juice, and beer. Simmer until reduced by half. Stir in Clemson Blue Cheese, and whisk until well blended. Add mustard and remove from heat. Pour mustard into a jar, and let cool to room temperature. Cover and refrigerate.

Blue Tartar Sauce
Servings: 6

1 cup	Mayonnaise		1 Tbsp	Capers, chopped
1 tsp	Shallots, finely chopped		1 tsp	Lemon juice
1 Tbsp	Chives, finely chopped		1 dash	Hot sauce
1 tsp	Mustard		¼ cup	Clemson Blue Cheese crumbles
2 Tbsp	Sweet pickles, chopped			

Combine all ingredients. Chill before serving.

White Wine Butter Sauce with Clemson Blue Cheese
Servings: 4

2	Shallots, finely chopped		6 ounces	Cold butter (cut in pieces)
2 Tbsp	White vinegar		1 ounces	Clemson Blue Cheese crumbles
4 Tbsp	White wine		¼ tsp	Ground white pepper
3 Tbsp	Heavy cream			

Place shallots and vinegar in a small sauce pan, and reduce until almost gone. Add white wine and reduce until half gone (about 2 tablespoons). Add heavy cream and reduce again by ¼. Turn the heat to low, and whisk in the butter a little at a time; fully incorporate each piece before adding the next. Occasionally remove the pan from the heat to make sure it never boils. Whisk in Clemson Blue Cheese and white pepper. Serve with seafood, chicken, pork, or vegetables.

Clemson Blue Cheese Vegetable Pizza Sandwich
Servings: 6

2	Zucchini, thinly sliced		3	English muffins, split and toasted
2	Celery stalk, thinly sliced		6 ounces	Pizza sauce
2 small	Carrots, peeled and grated		3 Tbsp	Clemson Blue Cheese, crumbled
1 Tbsp	Olive oil			

Heat broiler. In a large skillet, sauté vegetables in olive oil until tender. Top each toasted muffin half with 2 tablespoons of pizza sauce, sautéed vegetables, and cheese. Broil 6 inches from heat, 4 to 6 minutes or until cheese melts.

Roast Beef and Clemson Blue Cheese Sandwich
Servings: 4 / Yield: ½ cup

8 ounces	Red bell peppers, roasted		1 pound	Roast beef, sliced thin
8 Tbsp	Herb mayonnaise (recipe follows)		2 ounces	Red onion, sliced thin
8 slices	White sourdough bread		12	Tomato slices
6 ounces	Clemson Blue Cheese, crumbled		4	Romaine lettuce leaves

HERB MAYONNAISE:

1 cup	Mayonnaise		1 tsp	Fresh cilantro, chopped
1 Tbsp	Fresh basil, chopped		1 tsp	Fresh parsley, chopped

Slice peppers into strips ¼-inch wide. To assemble one sandwich, spread 2 tablespoons of herb mayonnaise on a slice of bread, and top with 1 leaf of romaine lettuce and 1½ ounces of Clemson Blue Cheese. Then place 4 ounces of roast beef on top of the lettuce, and cover with ½ ounce of red onions, 2 ounces of red bell peppers strips, and 3 tomato slices. Top with a slice of bread. To make the Herb Mayonnaise: Stir all ingredients together until the herbs are evenly distributed throughout the mayonnaise. Chill until ready to use.

Chicken and Clemson Blue Cheese Salad Croissant
Servings: 4

2 cups	Cooked chicken, diced		4	Croissants, split and toasted
1	Avocado, peeled and cubed		4 slices	Bacon, cooked crisp
¼ cup	Mayonnaise		4	Romaine leaves
¼ cup	Clemson Blue Cheese, crumbled		1 medium	Tomato, sliced
2	Hard-boiled eggs, peeled and chopped		2 Tbsp	Alfalfa sprouts

In a medium bowl, combine chicken, avocado, mayonnaise, Clemson Blue Cheese, and eggs. Spoon mixture onto bottom of each croissant, and top with bacon, lettuce leaf, tomato, alfalfa sprouts, and croissant top.

Caramelized Onion, Pear, and Clemson Blue Cheese Panini
Servings: 4

2 ounces	Butter	2	Pears, cored and sliced
1 medium	Onion, thinly sliced	4 ounces	Clemson Blue Cheese, crumbled
8 slices	Whole grain bread	4 Tbsp	Olive oil
2 cups	Arugula		

In a small sauté pan, melt butter; add onion slices and sauté until golden brown (about 10 minutes).

Assemble sandwiches by layering arugula, sautéed onions, pears, and Clemson Blue Cheese on 4 pieces of bread. Top with remaining bread slices. Brush sandwiches with olive oil. Grill or pan-fry sandwiches on both sides, or toast in a panini grill until golden brown. Cut each sandwich in ½ and serve.

Turkey and Tomato Cobb Wrap
Servings: 4

4 large	Flour tortillas, (10-inch)	2 medium	Tomatoes, sliced
6 Tbsp	Clemson Blue Cheese dressing (on pg. 42)	8 ounces	Turkey breast, cooked and sliced
		8 leaves	Boston, iceberg or leaf lettuce
1	Avocado, peeled and thinly sliced	4 strips	Bacon, cooked crisp

Spread each tortilla with 1½ tablespoons of the dressing. Top with layers of turkey, tomato, lettuce, avocado, and reserved bacon, dividing evenly. Roll up tortillas. If desired, tie each wrap with chives, or secure with long toothpicks; cut ⅓ from an end. On a serving plate, stand both portions of the wrap on the cut ends. Repeat with remaining wraps.

Turkey and Clemson Blue Cheese Baguette Sandwich

For each sandwich, use $\frac{1}{6}$ of a freshly baked French baguette, split horizontally. Spread the cut side of both top and bottom with a thin layer of Clemson Blue Cheese spread.

On the bottom part, layer arugula, baby spinach, or spring mix lettuce. Top with sliced tomato and thinly sliced roasted turkey.

Cover with the top part of the baguette.

Clemson Blue Cheese Baked Shrimp
Servings: 6

12 ounces	Cream cheese	½ cup	Whole milk
4 ounces	Clemson Blue Cheese, crumbled	2 Tbsp	Lemon juice
¼ tsp	Tabasco sauce	2 pounds	Large shrimp, peeled and deveined

In a mixing bowl, combine cream cheese, Clemson Blue Cheese, and Tabasco sauce. Add milk and lemon juice; stirring until smooth. Add shrimp and toss until well coated. Place shrimp individually on a greased baking sheet. Bake in a 350F oven until very hot and light brown (about 8 minutes). TIP: Serve over rice or pasta.

Flounder with Spinach, Pine Nuts, and Clemson Blue Cheese
Servings: 4

8	Flounder fillets, boneless and skinless, approximate 2 ounces each	4 ounces	Clemson Blue Cheese, crumbled
		½ tsp	Ground white pepper
4 ounces	Cooked spinach	1 ounces	Butter
¼ cup	Pine nuts, toasted	⅓ cup	White wine

In a mixing bowl, combine spinach, pine nuts, Clemson Blue Cheese, and white pepper.
Lay the flounder fillets on a board, skin-side up. Divide the spinach mixture between the fillets, and roll up the fish from head to tail. Butter an ovenproof dish, and place the flounder fillets in it, standing them on their sides like a turban. Pour wine over and cover loosely with a sheet of aluminum foil. Bake in a 375F oven for 15–20 minutes until fish is cooked through.

Shrimp, Clemson Blue Cheese, and Grits
Servings: 4

1 ounce	Butter	2 tsp	Blackening spice
4 tsps	Garlic, chopped	4 tsps	Scallions, chopped
4 tsps	Shallots, chopped	⅔ cup	Sherry
1 cup	Diced tasso ham	1 cup	Heavy cream
4 Tbsp	Tomatoes, chopped	2 ounces	Clemson Blue Cheese, crumbled
40 pieces	Shrimp (21 to 26 per pound), peeled and deveined		Salt and pepper to taste

In a large sauté pan, heat butter, and add garlic and shallots: sauté 1 minute. Add tasso ham, scallions, and tomatoes; sauté for another minute. Add blackening spice and shrimp; sauté for an additional minute, and add sherry to deglaze the pan. Pour in heavy cream and bring to a boil; remove shrimp and reduce cream to a sauce-like, thick consistency. Add shrimp and Clemson Blue Cheese. Salt and pepper to taste. Place 1 cup of cooked grits in individual bowls, and pour shrimp mixture over grits.

Clemson Blue Cheese Baked Mahi-Mahi
Servings: 1

Coat a 5–6 ounce boneless/skinless mahi-mahi fillet in olive oil, and place it on a sheet pan or sauté pan. Sprinkle crumpled Clemson Blue Cheese over it.

Bake in a 350F oven until it reaches an internal temperature of 145F (about 10 minutes).

Bacon-Wrapped Chicken Breast with Cashews and Clemson Blue Cheese
Servings: 4

4	Chicken breast, boneless, skinless, and about 4–5 ounces each	2 Tbsp	Butter
		2 Tbsp	Flour
½ cup	Clemson Blue Cheese, crumbled	1 cup	Chicken stock
¼ cup	Cashews, roasted, chopped	¼ cup	Heavy cream
2	Green onions, chopped	2 Tbsp	Grainy mustard
¼ tsp	Ground white pepper	Salt and pepper	
8 slices	Bacon		

Place chicken breasts flat on a cutting board, and make a pocket by cutting a horizontally from the side but not all the way through. In a small mixing bowl, combine Clemson Blue Cheese, cashews, green onions, and pepper. Stuff chicken breasts with the cheese mixture in equal amounts, and wrap each chicken breast in 2 slices of bacon, leaving the ends of the bacon on the underside if possible. Place the chicken breasts on a baking sheet and bake in a 375-degree oven until done (165F internal temperature) and the bacon is crisp, about 20 to 25 minutes.

In a small sauce pot, melt butter and whisk in flour. Cook for 2 minutes and whisk in chicken stock. Simmer for 6 to 8 minutes, and add heavy cream; continue simmering for another few minutes until thick and smooth; add mustard, and salt and pepper to taste. To serve, ladle sauce onto each plate, and top with a chicken breast.

Sautéed Chicken Breast with Creamy Clemson Blue Cheese Sauce
Servings: 4

2 Tbsp	Olive oil	1 cup	Clemson Blue Cheese, crumbled
4	Chicken breasts, boneless skinless, and about 4–6 ounces each	¾ cup	Heavy cream
		¼ tsp	Ground white pepper
⅓ cup	White wine	1 Tbsp	Tarragon, chopped

In a medium-sized skillet, heat olive oil over medium heat. Add chicken breasts (skin-side down), and cook (about 3 minutes). Turn chicken over, and cook another 3 minutes.

Reduce the heat down and add white wine; simmer for 7 to 8 minutes until wine has reduced by half. Add Clemson Blue Cheese, cream, pepper, and chopped tarragon. Bring again to a simmer, and then put the skillet in a 350-degree oven for 12 to 15 minutes or until chicken is done and the sauce has thickened lightly.

Chicken with Shiitake and Clemson Blue Cheese Sauce
Servings: 4

3 Tbsp	Vegetable oil	12 ounces	Shiitake mushroom, sliced
4	Chicken breasts, boneless, skinless, and about 4-6 ounces each	½ cup	White wine
		¾ cup	Heavy cream
1 cup	Flour	½ cup	Clemson Blue Cheese, crumbled
3 Tbsp	Butter	1 Tbsp	Parsley, chopped
1	Shallot, chopped		Salt and pepper

Heat vegetable oil in a large ovenproof skillet over medium-high heat. Coat chicken in flour; shake off excess, and sauté in skillet until golden (about 1 minute per side). Place skillet in 375-degree oven until chicken is cooked through, about 12 to 15 minutes. Melt butter in a sauce pan over moderate heat; add shallots and shiitake mushrooms. Sauté until soft, add wine, and simmer until reduced by half. Add cream and reduce until slightly thickened. Add Clemson Blue Cheese and simmer until cheese is melted and sauce is smooth. Season with salt and pepper. Spoon shiitake and Clemson Blue Cheese sauce onto 4 large dinner plates. Slice chicken diagonally, and place atop sauce. Sprinkle with chopped parsley.

Meatloaf with Buffalo Sauce and Clemson Blue Cheese

Servings: 4

1½ pounds	Ground beef		2 tsp	Worcestershire sauce
½ cup	Salsa, mild		½ tsp	Ground pepper
½ cup	Bread crumbs		1 tsp	Dry mustard
1 small	Onion, chopped		1 tsp	Salt
1 large	Egg		¼ cup	Milk

SAUCE:

⅓ cup	Hot pepper sauce		½ tsp	Garlic powder
⅓ cup	Melted butter or oil		2 Tbsp	Worcestershire sauce
2 tsp	Lemon juice			

TOPPING:

½ cup	Clemson Blue Cheese crumbles

In a large mixing bowl, combine ground beef, salsa, bread crumbs, and diced onions. Add egg, 2 teaspoons Worcestershire sauce, salt, dry mustard, 1 teaspoon garlic powder, and pepper. Slowly pour in milk, and mix well.

For the sauce: Combine hot sauce, melted butter, lemon juice, ½ teaspoon garlic powder, and 2 tablespoons Worcestershire sauce. Mix until well incorporated.

Place meat mixture in a baking pan, loaf pan, or in large individual muffin pans. Pour buffalo sauce over, and sprinkle with Clemson Blue Cheese. Bake in a 350F oven until internal temperature reaches 165F or about 45 minutes if baked in a baking dish or loaf pan (less time if baked in muffin pans).

Beef Tips in Beer and Clemson Blue Cheese

Servings: 4

¼ cup	Vegetable oil		½ cup	Beef broth
2 pounds	Beef tips		1	Red bell pepper, seeded and sliced
3 Tbsp	All-purpose flour		4 ounces	Clemson Blue Cheese, crumbled
8 ounces	Mushrooms, sliced		¼ cup	Parsley, chopped
2 Tbsp	Tomato paste		1 tsp	Ground pepper
2 cups	Dark beer			

Heat oil in a large skillet. Toss meat in flour, and brown in the skillet in 2 to 3 batches. Transfer meat with a slotted spoon to a casserole dish. Cook mushrooms in the same skillet, and add tomato paste, beer, and beef broth. Bring to a boil and pour over beef. Place casserole in a 375-degree oven for 1 hour. Add peppers, Clemson Blue Cheese, parsley, and pepper, and continue cooking for another 20 minutes until meat is tender. **TIP: Serve over mashed potatoes.**

Clemson Blue Cheese Stuffed Steak with Mushrooms
Servings: 4

4	New York strip steaks, 8 ounces each	2 cups	Mushroom, sliced
⅓ cup	Clemson Blue Cheese crumbles	1 tsp	Dried thyme
1 tsp	Black pepper	⅓ cup	Red wine
1 Tbsp	Olive oil		Salt and pepper
1 tsp	Garlic, chopped		

Place steaks on a flat surface, and with a sharp knife, carefully cut a horizontal pocket through the middle of steak; do not cut all the way through. Fill pocket with Clemson Blue Cheese. Secure open end with skewers or tooth picks if desired. Season with pepper, and grill until desired doneness. While the steaks are grilling, heat a medium-sized skillet over medium-high heat. Add oil, and when hot, add garlic and then mushrooms. Sauté until mushrooms are tender, and then pour in red wine and cook until all liquid has been absorbed. Season with salt and pepper. To serve, place steaks on a platter, and top with mushrooms.

Clemson Blue Cheese Pork Chops
Servings: 4

1 Tbsp	Vegetable oil	½ tsp	Granulated garlic
1 Tbsp	Butter	¼ cup	White wine
4	Pork chops, 8 ounces each	1 cup	Heavy cream
½ tsp	Ground black pepper	2 ounces	Clemson Blue Cheese crumbles

In a large skillet or frying pan, heat oil and butter over high heat until butter turns golden brown. Season pork chops with pepper and garlic, and add them to the pan. Turn down heat, and cook (about 6 minutes). Turn the pork chops, sprinkle with salt, and cook to an internal temperature of 145F, turning occasionally to brown evenly. Remove pork chops from the skillet, keep them warm, and leave them to rest. Add white wine to the skillet, loosening any bits of meat. Add heavy cream and cook. Stir occasionally until sauce starts to thicken. Stir in Clemson Blue Cheese, and cook until cheese is melted and the sauce is thick and smooth. Spoon sauce over pork chops.

Creamy Clemson Blue Cheese Bacon Burgers
Servings: 8

8	Hamburgers, grilled	1 cup	Clemson Blue Cheese, crumbled
4 slices	Bacon, diced	2 Tbsp	Parsley, chopped
1 cup	Onion, chopped	½ tsp	Ground black pepper
½ cup	Sour cream	8	Hamburger buns, toasted

In a medium skillet, cook bacon until crisp; add onions and cook until onions are golden brown, stirring occasionally. In a medium-sized bowl, combine sour cream, Clemson Blue Cheese, parsley, and pepper. Stir in bacon and onions. Arrange burgers on buns, and top with mixture of Clemson Blue Cheese, bacon and onion.

◀ Clemson Blue Cheese Tenderloin Steaks
Servings: 4

4	Beef tenderloin steaks, 1-inch thick
1 large	Garlic clove, halved
2 tsp	Fresh parsley, chopped

CHEESE TOPPING:

2 Tbsp	Cream cheese, softened		4 tsp	Yogurt, plain
4 tsp	Clemson Blue Cheese, crumbled		2 tsp	Onion, minced
1 dash	Salt			

Rub each side of beef steaks with garlic. Place steaks on grill. Grill 3 to 4 minutes. Turn and season with ¼ teaspoon salt, and grill 3 to 4 minutes. In small bowl, combine topping ingredients, and top each steak with an equal amount of cheese topping. Broil an additional 1 to 2 minutes. Garnish with parsley.

New York Strip Steaks with Clemson Blue Cheese
Servings: 4

4	New York strip steaks, 10–12 ounce each		10 ounces	Clemson Blue Cheese, crumbled
1 Tbsp	Vegetable oil		2 ounces	Butter, softened
1 Tbsp	Ground black pepper		2 Tbsp	Heavy cream

Heat the grill to medium high. Brush the steaks with oil, and season with pepper. Grill steaks to the desired doneness. In a small mixing bowl, combine Clemson Blue Cheese, butter, and cream. Divide cheese mixture onto the steaks; remove steaks from the heat, and let rest 5 to 10 minutes before serving.

Clemson Blue Cheese Meatballs
Servings: 6

2 pounds	Ground beef		2 Tbsp	Worcestershire sauce
1 cup	Clemson Blue Cheese, crumbled		3 ounces	Butter
¼ cup	Onion, finely chopped		1 cup	Heavy cream
1	Egg		¼ cup	Chopped parsley
1 tsp	Ground white pepper			

In a large mixing bowl, combine beef, Clemson Blue Cheese, onion, egg, white pepper, and Worcestershire sauce. Roll mixture into 24 meatballs. In a large skillet, melt butter over high heat. Add meatballs (in 2 batches if necessary), and brown on all sides. Cover meatballs, reduce heat to low, and cook 5 to 7 minutes until done. Place meatballs in a serving platter. Add parsley to skillet and then heavy cream. Increase the heat to medium, and reduce the heavy cream until it is slightly thickened (about 3 to 4 minutes). Add salt and pepper to sauce, if necessary, and pour over meatballs.

Ribeye Steaks with Clemson Blue Cheese and Blueberry Vinaigrette
Servings: 8

8	Rib eye steaks, 10–12 ounce each	1 Tbsp	Honey
1 cup	Clemson Blue Cheese, crumbled	½ cup	Balsamic vinegar
1 Tbsp	Butter	1 cup	Walnut oil
1	Shallot, finely chopped		Salt and pepper
1 clove	Garlic, finely chopped		Pinch cinnamon
½ cup	Blueberries		

Grill rib eye steaks to desired doneness. Sprinkle Clemson Blue Cheese on top of steak. In a small saucepan, melt butter and add shallots and garlic; cook for 1 minute. Add blueberries, honey, and vinegar, and bring to a boil. Transfer to a food processor and purée; slowly add oil, salt, pepper, and cinnamon. Drizzle vinaigrette over steaks and serve.

Oven-Roasted Pork Loin with Clemson Blue Cheese Sauce
Servings: 6

2½ pound	Pork loin	¼ cup	White wine
1 Tbsp	Vegetable oil	½ cup	Sour cream
1 tsp	Ground pepper	4 ounces	Clemson Blue Cheese, crumbled

Brush pork loin in vegetable oil, and sprinkle with ground pepper. Roast in a 350-degree oven until it reaches an internal temperature of 145F. Keep the roast warm, and let it rest while making the sauce. Pour 2 tablespoons of fat from the roasting pan into a small sauce pot. Add white wine and bring it to a boil, stirring. Reduce heat and stir in sour cream and Clemson Blue Cheese. Stir until cheese has melted, but do not allow it to boil. Adjust seasoning. Carve the roast into thin slices, and pour the sauce over, or serve it separately.

Clemson Cheeseburgers with Pancetta
Servings: 4

2 pounds	Ground sirloin or chuck	2 Tbsp	Unsalted butter, melted
8	Pancetta, thinly sliced		Romaine lettuce leaves
4 ounces	Clemson Blue Cheese		Tomato slices
4	Hamburger buns or Kaiser rolls, split		Freshly ground pepper
1	Sweet onion, extra thin slices		

Shape the meat into 4 patties, and season on both sides with pepper. Wrap each hamburger with 2 slices of pancetta. Grill the burgers over a medium-hot fire (about 4 minutes) or until nicely browned on the bottom. Flip the burgers and top them with the Clemson Blue Cheese. Grill for about 4 minutes longer or until cooked through. Meanwhile, brush the cut sides of the buns with the butter, and grill them, cut-side down, until lightly toasted. Set the burgers on the bun bottoms, and top with lettuce, tomato, and onion. Serve immediately.

The Blue Tiger Burger

In a mixing bowl, make a sauce by combining 1 cup mayonnaise, ⅔ cup ketchup, ¼ cup yellow mustard, 1 teaspoon paprika, ½ teaspoon curry, ¼ teaspoon white pepper, and 1 teaspoon salt. This will make 2 cups of sauce.

For each person, make two 3–4-ounce thin beef patties. Sprinkle Clemson Blue Cheese crumbles on one of them, place the other patty on top of the Clemson Blue Cheese, and gently press the 2 patties together. Grill to your preferred doneness.

Grill sliced onion, sliced tomatoes, and hamburger bun along with the Clemson Blue Cheese burgers.

Serve open-faced, with sauce and burger on the bottom bun with; sprinkle more Clemson Blue Cheese on top if you like. Place lettuce, onion, and tomato on top bun (Close it for a more traditional burger). Add pickles, cooked bacon or mushrooms if you prefer.

Clemson Blue Cheese Burgers
Servings: 4

1½ pound	Ground beef	3 ounces	Clemson Blue Cheese, crumbled
2 Tbsp	Dijon mustard	1 large	Egg
1 tsp	Granulated garlic		Salt and pepper
3	Green onions, chopped		

In a large bowl, combine ground beef, mustard, granulated garlic, green onions, Clemson Blue Cheese, and egg, and mix until just incorporated. Shape mixture into 4 patties. Sauté, grill, or broil patties to your desired doneness. Sprinkle with salt and pepper.

Grilled Clemson Blue Cheese Lamb Patties
Servings: 4

1½ pound	Ground lamb	3 Tbsp	Ketchup
¼ cup	Onion, finely chopped	2 tsp	Worcestershire sauce
½ cup	Crumbled Clemson Blue Cheese, divided	½ tsp	Pepper

In a mixing bowl, combine lamb, onion, ketchup, Worcestershire sauce, and pepper. Shape into 8 thin patties. Place 1 tablespoon Clemson Blue Cheese on each of the patties. Cover with remaining 4 patties; seal edges. Grill 6 to 8 minutes; turn and grill 4 minutes or until internal temperature reaches 155F. Top with remaining Clemson Blue Cheese.

Pan-Roasted Strip Steak over Clemson Blue Cheese Onions
Servings: 6

6	Strip steaks or ribeye steaks, 10 ounce each	2	Green onions, chopped
2 Tbsp	Butter	½ tsp	Dried thyme
2 large	Onions, sliced	⅓ cup	Clemson Blue Cheese, crumbled
2 Tbsp	Honey	1 tsp	Ground white pepper
2 ounces	Smoked ham, chopped	1 Tbsp	Ground black pepper
1 cup	Heavy cream	2 Tbsp	Vegetable oil
			Salt to taste

In a large sauté pan, melt butter over moderate heat. Add onions and sauté until translucent (about 4 minutes); add honey and ham. Cook for another 4 minutes, stirring occasionally. Add cream, green onions, and thyme, and reduce until lightly thickened (about 5 minutes). Stir in Clemson Blue Cheese and white pepper, and simmer until cheese is melted and the sauce is smooth. In a large skillet or frying pan, heat oil over high heat. Sprinkle black pepper over the steaks, and add them to the pan. Turn the heat down to medium, and cook for about 4 minutes. Turn the meat, sprinkle with salt, and cook to your preferred doneness (about 4 more minutes for medium rare). Transfer the steaks to a platter, and leave them to rest in a warm place for approximately 5 minutes. Cut each steak diagonally into ½-inch slices. Reheat the sauce, if necessary, and spoon it onto warmed plates. Top with the sliced steaks.

Potato and Clemson Blue Cheese Ravioli
Servings: 1 / Yield: 12 Raviolis

1 small	Baking potato (about ½ pound)	2 Tbsp	Heavy cream
2 ounce	Clemson Blue Cheese, crumbled	24	Wonton wrappers
2	Scallions, cut in thin slices	Salt and pepper	

Boil potato in water until done (about 20 minutes). Drain and peel potato, and place in a small mixing bowl. Mash potato and add Clemson Blue Cheese, scallion, heavy cream, salt, and pepper. Mix thoroughly. Lay half of the wonton wrappers on a flat work surface, and brush them lightly with water. Put about 1 tablespoon of the potato mixture in the center of each. Top each with the remaining wrappers, and press around the edges to seal, taking care not to leave any air pockets inside. With a cookie cutter, stamp out the ravioli. Press firmly around the edges with a fork to make sure they are sealed. Cook the ravioli in a pot of salted boiling water until done (about 3 minutes). Remove ravioli with a slotted spoon; drain.

Orzo with Cherry Tomatoes, Herbs, and Clemson Blue Cheese
Servings: 4

3 Tbsp	Olive oil	1 cup	Chicken stock
½ medium	Onion, chopped	2 cups	Cherry tomato, halved
2 clove	Garlic, minced	1 tsp	Basil, chopped
1 cup	Orzo pasta	1 tsp	Tarragon, chopped
¼ cup	White wine	2 ounces	Clemson Blue Cheese, crumbled

In a saucepan, heat olive oil. Add onion and garlic, and sauté for 1 minute. Add orzo, stirring, for another minute; add white wine and chicken stock. Cover and simmer over low heat until orzo is done (about 12 minutes). Add tomatoes and herbs, and toss. Season with salt and pepper; serve in pasta bowls, and sprinkle Clemson Blue Cheese on top.

Orzo with Caramelized Onions and Clemson Blue Cheese
Servings: 4

⅓ cup	Vegetable oil	4 ounces	Cream cheese
3 large	Onions, sliced	2 cups	Spinach, chopped
1 pound	Orzo pasta	Salt and pepper	
8 ounces	Clemson Blue Cheese, crumbled		

Heat oil in a large skillet over low heat, and add onions. Cook about 20 minutes, stirring until golden brown. While onions are cooking, bring a large pot of lightly salted water to a boil and add orzo; cook until al dente (about 8 minutes). Drain. Remove onion skillet from the heat, and add Clemson Blue Cheese and cream cheese; mix well. Add spinach, pasta, salt, and pepper; toss to combine.

◀ Mac and Clemson Blue Cheese
Servings: 8

1 pound	Elbow macaroni		3 cups	Half and half
3 Tbsp	Butter		3 cups	Cheddar cheese, grated
¼ cup	Flour		1½ cups	Clemson Blue Cheese, crumbled

Cook pasta in boiling water until al dente (about 8 minutes) and drain. Butter an oven-safe dish (13 x 9 x 2) with 1 tablespoon butter. Melt 2 tablespoons butter in a sauce pan over low heat, add flour, and stir for about 1 minute without browning. Add cream. Simmer until the sauce thickens slightly (about 3 minutes), stirring occasionally. Add grated cheddar cheese and one cup of Clemson Blue Cheese; whisk until cheeses melt. Add pasta to sauce and stir to coat. Transfer pasta to prepared baking dish, and sprinkle with remaining Clemson Blue Cheese. Bake in 350-degree oven until sauce begins to bubble (about 25 minutes).

Clemson Blue Cheese Fettuccine
Servings: 4

1 pound	Fettuccine		¾ cup	Chicken stock
4 Tbsp	Olive oil		½ cup	Clemson Blue Cheese, crumbled
¾ cup	Green onion, chopped		½ tsp	Ground white pepper
1½ cups	Mushrooms, sliced		¼ cup	Parmesan cheese, grated
2 Tbsp	Lemon juice			

Cook fettuccine in a large pot of boiling, lightly salted water until al dente. Drain and keep warm. Heat oil in a large skillet; add green onions and mushrooms. Simmer for 4 to 5 minutes until mushrooms are soft. Add lemon juice, chicken stock, and Clemson Blue Cheese. Cook, stirring, until cheese is melted and the sauce is thickened. Add fettuccine and pepper. Toss to mix well. Arrange pasta on serving plates, and sprinkle with Parmesan cheese.

Linguine with Prosciutto Ham and Clemson Blue Cheese
Servings: 4

1 pound	Linguine		¾ cup	Chicken stock
1 Tbsp	Olive oil		4 ounces	Clemson Blue Cheese
2	Shallots, chopped		2 Tbsp	Parsley, chopped
6 ounces	Prosciutto, cut in ¼-inch strips		Salt and pepper to taste	
½ cup	Roasted red pepper, cut in strips			

Cook the linguine in a large pot of salted boiling water until al dente. Drain the pasta and return it to the pot; cover partially to keep warm. In a large sauté pan, heat the olive oil. Add shallots and sauté for 1 minute, add prosciutto ham and roasted red peppers, sauté for another minute, and stir in chicken stock. Simmer for 5 minutes, and add Clemson Blue Cheese. Stir until creamy; add parsley. Add salt and pepper to taste. Pour the sauce over the pasta, and toss well.

Buffalo Chicken Lasagna
Servings: 8

12 pieces	Lasagna sheets, uncooked	3 Tbsp	Hot sauce
¼ cup	Olive oil	2 Tbsp	Vinegar
1 pound	Chicken breasts, skinless, boneless and diced	1 tsp	Garlic salt
		1 pound	Ricotta cheese
4 cups	Spaghetti sauce	4	Eggs
1½ cups	White wine	1 cup	Clemson Blue Cheese, crumbled

Pour oil into a large skillet, and place it over medium-high heat until hot. Add chicken; sauté 4 minutes. Drain well. Stir in spaghetti sauce, wine, hot sauce, vinegar, and garlic salt. In a small bowl, combine ricotta cheese and eggs. Set aside. Spray a 9 × 13-inch baking pan with cooking spray. Spread 1 cup of the sauce over the bottom of the pan. Arrange 4 pieces of lasagna (3 lengthwise, 1 width wise) over the sauce. Cover with 1½ cups of the sauce. Spread half the ricotta mixture on top. Arrange another 4 pieces of lasagna over ricotta, and top with another 1½ cups of sauce. Spread remaining ricotta mixture on top. Arrange final 4 pieces of lasagna over ricotta mixture, and cover with remaining sauce. Heat oven to 350F. Cover lasagna with foil and bake for 1 hour and 10 minutes. Uncover lasagna, sprinkle Clemson Blue Cheese on top, and bake an additional 5 minutes uncovered. Cover and let stand 15 minutes before serving.

Buffalo Chicken Pasta ▶
Servings: 8

1 pound	Chicken breasts, boneless, skinless, cut into ½-inch pieces	2 tsp	Hot sauce
		1 cup	Sliced celery
1 pound	Penne pasta, uncooked	½ cup	Red onion, chopped
1 tsp	Paprika	1 cup	Mayonnaise
½ tsp	Salt	⅓ cup	Clemson Blue Cheese crumbles
½ tsp	Garlic powder	¾ cup	Half and half
½ tsp	Black pepper	3 Tbsp	Clemson Blue Cheese, crumbled
2 tsp	Vegetable oil		

Boil pasta in lightly oiled and salted water. While pasta is cooking, add oil to a large skillet and heat over medium-high heat. Add chicken to skillet, and sauté over medium-high heat; add paprika, salt, garlic powder, and pepper, stirring frequently. Add celery and onion, and sauté until chicken is golden brown and cooked through (about 4 minutes). Add hot sauce. Cook for 1 minute. Combine mayonnaise, ⅓ cup Clemson Blue Cheese and half and half in a small bowl. Add to chicken and vegetables in skillet. Stir constantly and cook over medium-low heat until thoroughly heated. When pasta is done, drain and return to pot. Add contents of skillet to pot, and mix well. Transfer to serving dish, and sprinkle with 3 tablespoons Clemson Blue Cheese. Serve immediately.

Fettuccine with Pancetta and Clemson Blue Cheese

Servings: 4

1 pound	Fettuccine		½ tsp	Crushed red pepper
2 Tbsp	Olive oil		¾ cup	Chicken stock
2	Shallots, thinly sliced		¼ pound	Clemson Blue Cheese
1 slice	Pancetta (¼-inch thick), julienned		2 Tbsp	Parsley, finely chopped
½ cup	Oil-packed sun-dried tomatoes, drained, cut into thin strips			Freshly ground black pepper
				Salt

In a large pot of boiling, salted water, cook the fettuccine until al dente. Drain the pasta. Return the pasta to the pot, toss with 1 tablespoon olive oil, cover partially, and keep warm. Meanwhile, heat 1 tablespoon olive oil in a large skillet. Add the shallots and cook over moderately high heat for 1 minute. Stir in the pancetta and sun-dried tomatoes. Season with crushed red pepper, salt, and black pepper; cook for 3 minutes. Add ¼ cup of the chicken stock, and stir up any browned bits clinging to the bottom of the pan. Add the remaining ½ cup chicken stock and the Clemson Blue Cheese to the skillet, and stir over moderate heat until creamy. Pour the sauce over the pasta, add the parsley, and toss well. Serve at once.

◀ Bacon and Clemson Blue Cheese Quiche
Servings: 6

1 (9-inch)	Unbaked pie shell		¾ cup	Half and half
1 tsp	Oil		1 pinch	White pepper
6 ounces	Bacon, diced		1 pinch	Nutmeg
½ cup	Onion, chopped		¾ cup	Clemson Blue Cheese
3	Eggs			

Bake pie shell in a 350-degree oven for 5 minutes. In a medium sauté pan, cook the bacon in the oil until lightly browned. Add chopped onions, and cook until onions are tender. Drain the bacon fat. Whisk together eggs, half and half, pepper, and nutmeg. Scatter the bacon and Clemson Blue Cheese evenly over the pie crust. Slowly pour the egg mixture over. Bake on a sheet pan in a 350-degree oven for 35 to 40 minutes or until a knife inserted in the middle comes out clean.

Eggs Baked with Clemson Blue Cheese
Servings: 4

4	Eggs		4 Tbsp	Clemson Blue Cheese crumbles
4 Tbsp	Swiss cheese, grated		½ tsp	Ground white pepper
1 cup	Heavy whipping cream		2 Tbsp	Butter

Butter a small ovenproof dish. Sprinkle grated Swiss cheese over the bottom. Crack the eggs over the cheese, and cover with heavy cream. Sprinkle the Clemson Blue Cheese and pepper over the cream; dot with butter. Bake in a 325-degree oven for 15 minutes.

Ham and Clemson Blue Cheese Omelet
Servings: 1

3	Eggs		1 tsp	Olive oil
1 tsp	Cream		2 ounces	Ham, diced
1 dash	Ground white pepper		1 ounce	Clemson Blue Cheese crumbles

In a small bowl, lightly whisk together eggs, cream, and ground white pepper. Pour oil into an 8-inch, non-stick frying pan over medium heat. Add egg mixture, and using a wooden or high heat rubber spatula, stir and scrape the eggs while swirling the pan until small curds begin to form. Add ham and Clemson Blue Cheese. Remove the pan from the heat, and use the spatula to fold ⅓ of the omelet over the middle. Roll the omelet over one more time; tilt the pan and roll the omelet onto a dish, seam-side down.

Eggs Bleudict
Servings: 2

2	English muffins, split and toasted	½ tsp	Curry powder
1 Tbsp	Olive oil	¼ cup	Clemson Blue Cheese crumbles
4 slices	Canadian bacon	1 Tbsp	Chives, chopped
4	Eggs		

Heat olive oil in a medium skillet over medium heat. Add Canadian bacon, sauté for 1 minute, and turn. Break 1 egg over each piece of Canadian bacon. Sprinkle curry, Clemson Blue Cheese, and chives over eggs; season with salt and pepper, and cover skillet. Reduce heat to low, and cook until egg white is set, about 4 minutes. Transfer eggs/bacon to English muffin half and serve.

Egg Sandwich with Bacon, Arugula, and Clemson Blue Cheese
Servings: 2

2	Ciabatta rolls, split and toasted	1 Tbsp	Red wine vinegar
2 slices	Bacon, cut in cubes	¼ cup	Clemson Blue Cheese crumbles
1 Tbsp	Shallots, minced	2 tsp	Unsalted butter
1 tsp	Dijon mustard	2	Eggs
1 cup	Baby arugula		Fresh ground pepper

In a small skillet, cook bacon until just crisp. Add shallots and cook for 1 minute, stirring. Add red wine vinegar and cook for 10 to 15 seconds. Remove skillet from heat, and stir in Dijon mustard. Add arugula and then toss. Divide arugula bacon mixture between each roll bottom. Top each with Clemson Blue Cheese. Reheat skillet over medium heat. Add butter; crack eggs into skillet. Cook eggs to desired doneness; add ground pepper. Place eggs on top of arugula. Place roll top on eggs.

Sausage and Clemson Blue Cheese Casserole
Servings: 6

3 cups	White bread, cubed	2 cups	Cream
1 cup	Clemson Blue Cheese crumbles	2 tsp	Dijon mustard
12 ounces	Sausage patties, cooked and diced	1 cup	Cheddar cheese, shredded
6	Eggs		

Lightly grease six 8-ounce ramekins or small baking dishes. Divide bread cubes among the ramekins, sprinkle with Clemson Blue Cheese, and top with sausage. In a medium bowl, whisk together eggs, cream, and mustard. Pour egg mixture over sausage mixture, and sprinkle with shredded cheddar cheese. Cover with foil, and chill ramekins for 8 hours, or overnight. Let stand at room temperature for 15 to 20 minutes. Bake in a 350-degree oven for 45 minutes, remove covers, and bake for an additional 15 minutes or until set and lightly browned.

Scrambled Eggs with Clemson Blue Cheese and Chives

In a small bowl, lightly beat 2 or 3 eggs per person. Add approximately 1 teaspoon milk or cream per egg, plus a pinch of pepper.

In a small sauté pan (non-stick pans work well), heat a little butter or oil over medium heat. Pour the egg mixture into the pan, and lower the heat. Using a wooden spoon or spatula, stir the eggs as they cook. Add 1 teaspoon Clemson Blue Cheese crumbles for each egg when the eggs are softly set; stir for another few seconds. Remove the pan from the heat; give a final stir, keeping the eggs fluffy and velvety. Serve as quickly as possible.

TASTES OF CLEMSON BLUE CHEESE
Vegetables & Sides

Clemson Blue Cheese Au Gratin Potatoes

Servings: 6

1½ pound	Baking potatoes, peeled and cut into ¼-inch slices	½ cup	Clemson Blue Cheese, crumbled
2 cloves	Garlic, minced	½ cup	Parmesan cheese, grated
1 Tbsp	Ground white pepper	1 cup	Half and half

In a large bowl, toss potatoes with garlic and pepper. Spray a baking dish with cooking spray, arrange a layer of potatoes in the bottom, and sprinkle some of the cheeses over them. Continue layering potatoes and cheeses, ending with potatoes. Pour cream over potatoes, and bake in a 350-degree oven for 1 hour or until potatoes are done.

Clemson Blue Cheese Baked Tomatoes

Servings: 6

6 medium	Tomatoes	4 slices	Bacon, cooked and crumbled
1½ cups	Clemson Blue Cheese salad dressing (on pg. 42)	⅓ cup	Green onions, chopped
		4 tsp	Parsley, chopped

Remove the flower stem from the bottom of tomatoes. At the other end, cut an X about half way through tomatoes. Place in a baking dish, cut-side up, and squish lightly on the sides to make an opening in the top. Pour approximately ¼-inch of water in the dish around tomatoes.

In a small bowl, combine Clemson Blue Cheese dressing and chopped green onions. Spoon mixture evenly over tomatoes, and bake in hot oven or broil for about 4 minutes or until bubbly and light brown. Remove from oven and sprinkle with bacon and parsley. TIP: Omit bacon for a vegetarian option.

Scalloped Sweet Potatoes with Leeks and Clemson Blue Cheese

Servings: 6

2 ounces	Butter	1 tsp	Ground white pepper
2 pounds	Sweet potato, peeled and sliced	½ tsp	Ground nutmeg
8 ounces	Leeks, white part only, sliced and washed well	6 ounces	Clemson Blue Cheese, crumbled
		1½ cups	Half and half

Butter a large rectangular baking dish. In a large mixing bowl, combine sweet potatoes, leeks, pepper, and nutmeg. Place ⅓ of the sweet potato/leeks mixture on the bottom of a buttered baking dish, and sprinkle with ⅓ of the Clemson Blue Cheese. Add another layer of potato/leeks and Clemson Blue Cheese. Add the remaining potato/leeks and Clemson Blue Cheese. Pour cream over top, and bake at 350F until potatoes are done (about 1 hour).

Baked Chipotle and Clemson Blue Cheese Grits ▶
Servings: 6

3 cups	Milk	3 large	Eggs
1 clove	Garlic, minced	ounces	Chipotle peppers, canned and chopped
1 cup	Quick-cooking grits	2 Tbsp	Parmesan cheese, grated
½ cup	Clemson Blue Cheese, crumbled	1 tsp	Dried oregano
⅓ cup	Butter	½ tsp	Ground pepper
½ cup	Heavy cream	1 tsp	Salt

In a sauce pot, bring milk and garlic to a boil, and slowly stir in grits. Reduce heat, cover, and simmer for 10 minutes. Whisk in Clemson Blue Cheese and butter. Add cream, eggs, chipotle peppers, oregano, pepper, and salt; whisk until all ingredients are well combined. Pour the mixture into a lightly greased 1½-quart ovenproof dish, and bake at 350F for 1 hour.

Baked Sweet Potato with Crumbled Clemson Blue Cheese
Servings: 4

4 medium	Sweet potatoes	4 Tbsp	Clemson Blue Cheese, crumbled
4 Tbsp	Butter	4 tsp	Chives, chopped

Thoroughly scrub sweet potatoes, and lightly prick potato skins with a fork. Bake at 400F until done, about 40 to 50 minutes. Cut a slit in potatoes, about ¾ of the length of each potato. Push in ends gently to open. Place 1 tablespoon of butter, 1 tablespoon of Clemson Blue Cheese crumbles, and 1 teaspoon of chopped chives in the opening of each potato. Serve immediately.

Cauliflower Fritters with Clemson Blue Cheese Sauce
Servings: 12

2 medium	Cauliflower heads, cut into florets	2	Shallots, chopped
2¾ cups	All-purpose flour	1 clove	Garlic, minced
12 ounces	Beer	¼ cup	White wine
¼ cup	Oil	2½ cups	Heavy cream
3	Eggs	1 cup	Clemson Blue Cheese, crumbled
1 pinch	Nutmeg	2 ounces	Butter
½ tsp	Salt	2 Tbsp	Chives, chopped
2 Tbsp	Butter	Salt and pepper	

Beer batter: In a large mixing bowl, combine flour, beer, oil, egg yolks, nutmeg, and salt. In a small mixing bowl, beat egg whites to soft peaks, and fold into flour mixture. Dip cauliflower florets into batter, and deep fry.

Sauce: In a sauce pot, melt 2 tablespoons butter, and add shallots and garlic. Sauté for 1 minute, add white wine, and reduce by half. Add cream and reduce by half. Add Clemson Blue Cheese, butter, and chives; salt and pepper to taste.

Twice-Baked Clemson Blue Cheese Potato

For each person, wash a large baking potato, and bake on a baking sheet in a 375-degee oven for about 60 minutes or until tender. Cool slightly for about 10 to 15 minutes.

Lay the potato flat on a table, and cut off a "lid." (If the potato is really big, cut it in half to serve two people.) Scoop the pulp out into a large bowl, leaving a ¼-inch thick shell.

Mash the potato pulp, and add Clemson Blue Cheese crumbles, shredded Parmesan cheese, and cooked bacon crumbles, about 1 tablespoon of each. Add 2 tablespoons sour cream, ½ tablespoon butter, 2 teaspoons chopped chives, and a pinch of nutmeg.

Spoon the potato-cheese mixture back into the potato shell, and place the potato back onto the baking sheet; bake in the oven for approximately 15 minutes or until heated through.

Baked Mashed Sweet Potatoes with Bacon and Clemson Blue Cheese
Servings: 6

6 medium	Sweet potatoes, peeled and cubed	6 slices	Bacon, cooked and chopped
6 ounces	Butter	1 cup	Clemson Blue Cheese, crumbled
1 tsp	White pepper		

Boil potatoes in unsalted water in a large pot until done. Drain and return potatoes to the pot; mash, add butter, and pepper. Place mashed potatoes in a baking dish; sprinkle with bacon and Clemson Blue Cheese. Bake in 350-degree oven until cheese is melted and bubbly (about 10 to 12 minutes).

Sweet Potatoes with Walnuts and Clemson Blue Cheese
Servings: 6

2 pounds	Sweet potato, peeled and cubed	½ cup	Walnuts, chopped
2 Tbsp	Vegetable oil	½ cup	Clemson Blue Cheese, crumbled
2 tsp	Dried thyme		Salt and pepper

Combine sweet potatoes and oil, and spread them out on a large sheet pan. Bake in a 400-degree oven for approximately 45 minutes or until tender and lightly brown. Sprinkle with walnuts and Clemson Blue Cheese, and bake for an additional 3 to 4 minutes. Transfer potatoes to a large bowl, and toss with salt and pepper to taste. Serve warm.

Potato and Clemson Blue Cheese Casserole
Servings: 6

6 large	Potatoes, peeled and cubed	½ cup	Clemson Blue Cheese, crumbled
½ cup	Butter	⅓ cup	Bread crumbs
½ cup	Flour		Salt and pepper
2 cups	Half and half		

Boil potatoes in lightly salted water for 8 to 10 minutes until tender but still firm. Drain and transfer to a casserole dish. In a medium saucepan, melt butter and whisk in flour. Add half and half; simmer for 15 to 20 minutes, stirring occasionally. Remove from heat, whisk in Clemson Blue Cheese, and season with salt and pepper to taste. Pour cream mixture over potatoes, and sprinkle breadcrumbs on top. Bake in a 375-degree oven for 25 minutes or until top is light brown.

Clemson Blue Cheese Stuffing for Pork Chops or Chicken Breasts
Servings: 8

½ cup	Clemson Blue Cheese, crumbled
⅛ tsp	White pepper
½ cup	Walnuts, chopped

Combine all ingredients. 2 tablespoons equal 1 serving (makes enough stuffing for 8 pork chops).

Clemson Blue Cheese and Rosemary Potatoes
Servings: 6

1½ pound	New potatoes, cut into wedges	2 tsp	Rosemary, chopped
3 Tbsp	Olive oil	¼ cup	Cayenne pepper
¼ cup	Clemson Blue Cheese, crumbled	2 Tbsp	Parsley, chopped

Boil potatoes in lightly salted water for 8 minutes and drain. In a large mixing bowl, combine olive oil, Clemson Blue Cheese, rosemary, and cayenne pepper. Add potatoes and toss to mix well. Pour potatoes onto a baking sheet, and bake in a 350-degree oven for 30 minutes. Remove from oven and sprinkle with parsley. Toss to mix well; pour into serving dish.

Honey Glazed Carrots with Clemson Blue Cheese
Servings: 8

2 pounds	Baby carrots	2 Tbsp	Brown sugar, packed
2 tsp	Salt	2 Tbsp	Lemon juice
4 Tbsp	Butter	⅓ cup	Clemson Blue Cheese, crumbled
¼ cup	Honey		

Place carrots in a medium sauce pot; cover with water and add salt. Boil slowly (about 10 minutes) or until tender. Drain and set aside. In a sauté pan, melt butter over medium heat. Add honey and brown sugar; cook while stirring until sugar is dissolved. Add lemon juice and stir in carrots, coating them well. Heat until carrots are hot and glazed. Add Clemson Blue Cheese and serve.

Roasted Clemson Blue Cheese Potatoes
Servings: 4

1 pound	Red potatoes, cut into wedges	⅓ cup	Clemson Blue Cheese, crumbled
1 Tbsp	Vegetable oil	6 ounces	Bacon, cooked and chopped
¼ tsp	Ground black pepper	⅓ cup	Cheddar cheese, shredded

In a mixing bowl, toss potatoes with oil. Sprinkle with pepper, and place potatoes in a baking dish. Bake at 400F for about 30 minutes or until potatoes are tender. In a small mixing bowl, combine Clemson Blue Cheese, bacon, and cheddar cheese. Sprinkle mixture over potatoes, and bake until cheeses are melted.

Potatoes in Clemson Blue Cheese Cream
Servings: 6

4 ounces	Clemson Blue Cheese, crumbled	2 tsp	Parsley, chopped
1½ cup	Heavy cream	1 tsp	Rosemary, chopped
1½ pound	New potatoes, cooked	1 tsp	Ground white pepper

Melt Clemson Blue Cheese and cream together in the top of a double boiler over simmering water. Stir until smooth and creamy. Remove from heat. Cut each potato into 4 wedges, and arrange in a buttered baking dish. Sprinkle with parsley, rosemary, and pepper. Pour cream mixture over the potatoes, and bake at 400F until golden brown (about 20 minutes).

Desserts

Baked Pears with Pecans and Clemson Blue Cheese
Servings: 4

2 Tbsp	Butter		¼ tsp	Salt
2 large	Pears (Bartlett, Bosc, or Anjou)		¼ tsp	Ground white pepper
½ cup	Pecan pieces, toasted		¼ tsp	Ground nutmeg
4 Tbsp	Brown sugar		2 ounces	Clemson Blue Cheese, crumbled
2 Tbsp	Butter, melted			

Butter a baking dish (9 x 13). Peel, cut in half, and core pears. Place them in the buttered baking dish, and bake in a 450-degree oven for 15 minutes. Turn pears and bake until soft and lightly browned (about 10 more minutes). Meanwhile, in a small mixing bowl, combine pecans, brown sugar, melted butter, salt, pepper, and nutmeg. Spoon pecan mixture over pear halves, and top with Clemson Blue Cheese. Return pears to oven, and bake until Clemson Blue Cheese starts to melt (about 4 to 5 minutes).

Clemson Blue Cheesecake with Walnuts
Servings: 16

2 Tbsp	Butter		3 Tbsp	Flour
1 cup	Cheese crackers, crushed		¼ cup	Salsa
16 ounces	Cream cheese		1 cup	Sour cream
10 ounces	Clemson Blue Cheese, crumbled		½ cup	Green onions, chopped
4	Eggs		½ cup	Walnuts, chopped

Butter an 8-inch springform pan and sprinkle cheese crackers on bottom and sides. In a mixing bowl combine cream cheese, Clemson Blue Cheese, eggs, flour, salsa, and sour cream. Fold in chopped green onions. Pour mixture into spring-form pan and sprinkle with walnuts. Bake in water bath at 300F for 1 hour, 15 minutes or until set. Turn off oven and slightly open door to cool cheesecake slowly. Refrigerate.

Clemson Blue Cheese, Green Peppercorn, and Brandy Cheesecake
Servings: 16 / Yield: 1 10-inch springform pan

½ cup	Graham cracker crumbs		1 tsp	Green peppercorns
4 tsp	Butter, melted		¼ cup	Brandy
2 pounds	Clemson Blue Cheese, crumbled		6	Eggs

In a small mixing bowl, combine Graham cracker crumbs and melted butter. Press into bottom of a 10-inch springform pan. To make the filling, combine Clemson Blue Cheese, green peppercorns, brandy, and eggs, and blend thoroughly. Pour batter on top of crust. Bake in a water bath at 300F for 1 hour, 30 minutes or until set. Turn off the oven, and open oven door slightly. Allow cheesecake to cool in the oven for 1 hour before removing. Refrigerate.

◀ Apple Pie with Clemson Blue Cheese
Servings: 8

3 pounds	Apples, peeled, cored, chopped (Granny Smith, Rome, or Gala)	1 Tbsp	Vanilla extract
		2	Ready-made pie crusts
2 Tbsp	Lemon juice	2 Tbsp	Butter, cut into small pieces
¾ cup	Sugar	¼ cup	Clemson Blue Cheese, crumbled
3 Tbsp	Cornstarch	1 Tbsp	Milk
1 Tbsp	Cinnamon	1	Egg yolk
¼ tsp	Nutmeg		

In a large mixing bowl, combine apples and lemon juice; add sugar, corn starch, cinnamon, nutmeg, and vanilla extract. Place one pie crust in a 9-inch pie pan. Pile apple mixture into the pie pan, mounding it in the middle. Dot with butter and sprinkle Clemson Blue Cheese over. Top apples with second pie crust; seal by pinching edges to fasten to bottom crust. Make a few cuts in the top crust to vent. In a small bowl, whisk together egg yolk and milk. Brush the crust with egg mixture. Bake in a 350F oven for 55 to 60 minutes or until golden brown.

Clemson Blue Cheese Baked Apples with Pecans
Servings: 4

1	Red Delicious apple, cored and sliced	4 ounces	Clemson Blue Cheese, crumbled
		¼ cup	Pecan pieces, toasted
1	Granny Smith apple, cored and sliced		Salt and pepper

Arrange apple slices on a baking sheet with parchment paper, and sprinkle Clemson Blue Cheese over the apples. Bake at 400F for 3 to 4 minutes (until Clemson Blue Cheese is just melted). Transfer to a serving tray, and sprinkle with pecans, salt, and pepper.

Clemson Blue Cheese Soufflé
Servings: 6

6	Eggs, separated	1 tsp	Balsamic vinegar
11 ounces	Cream cheese	½ Tbsp	White pepper
½ cup	Heavy cream	½ cup	Clemson Blue Cheese, crumbled

Heat oven to 375F. Place egg yolks, heavy cream, balsamic vinegar, and pepper in a food processor, and run until smooth. Add Clemson Blue Cheese and run until incorporated. Place mixture in a mixing bowl. In another mixing bowl, whip egg whites until stiff, and fold into the cheese mixture. Butter 1 large or 6 small soufflé cups, and pour the mixture in. Bake in oven until lightly brown and puffed (25 to 30 minutes for a large soufflé and approximately 15 to 20 minutes for a small one). Serve immediately. The outside edge should be firm and the center still soft. Serve with an assortment of lettuces, and crusty bread or rolls. TIP: Serve as an appetizer, as a light lunch, a cheese course in a formal dinner or in place of dessert.

No-Bake Savory Clemson Blue Cheesecake
Servings: 16

1 cup	Breadcrumbs, fine and dry	16 ounces	Ricotta cheese
4 Tbsp	Butter, melted	4 ounces	Clemson Blue Cheese, crumbled
½ cup	Mayonnaise	6 ounces	Parmesan cheese, grated
1 cup	Basil leaves, packed	½ cup	Toasted almonds, finely chopped
3 cloves	Garlic, chopped		

In a small mixing bowl, combine breadcrumbs and butter. Press mixture into bottom of a 9-inch springform pan. Refrigerate. In a food processor, combine mayonnaise, basil, and garlic. Blend until smooth. In a mixing bowl, combine ricotta cheese, Clemson Blue Cheese, and Parmesan cheese. Add mayonnaise mixture; mix well. Spread cheese mixture over breadcrumb crust. Refrigerate for at least 8 hours. Remove sides of springform pan, place cheesecake on a cake stand or platter, and press chopped almonds onto sides of cheesecake. **TIP: Serve with crackers, pita points or bread.**

Clemson Blue Cheese Bread Pudding
Servings: 12

2 ounces	Butter	3 cups	Heavy cream
1	Onion, chopped	1 tsp	Ground white pepper
1¼ pound	Day-old bread, cubed	1 tsp	Granulated garlic
12 ounces	Clemson Blue Cheese, crumbled	1 tsp	Dry mustard
12	Egg yolks		

Melt butter in a small sauté pan. Add onion and sauté until light brown, about 10 minutes. Arrange half the bread cubes in a baking pan (9 x 13). Sprinkle half the Clemson Blue Cheese and the sautéed onions over the bread. Top with remaining bread cubes and cheese. In a small mixing bowl, combine egg yolks, heavy cream, pepper, granulated garlic, and dry mustard. Pour mixture over bread cubes; cover dish with plastic wrap and then foil. Let soak for a minimum of 1 hour in the refrigerator. Bake in a 375-degree oven for 35 minutes. Remove foil and plastic wrap, and bake for an additional 15 minutes or until set and light brown on top. **TIP: Prepare this dish in individual dishes.**

Clemson Blue Cheese with Marinated
Strawberries and Pistachio Nuts
Servings: 6

¼ cup	Balsamic vinegar	12 ounces	Clemson Blue Cheese
1 tsp	Dijon mustard	1 cup	Fresh basil
⅔ cup	Olive oil	3 Tbsp	Pistachio nuts, chopped
1 pint	Strawberries, sliced	Salt and pepper	

In a small bowl, combine vinegar and mustard, whisk in olive oil, and add salt and pepper to taste. Add strawberries and marinate for 4-5 minutes. Cut Clemson Blue Cheese into wedges, and arrange with strawberries on plates. Garnish with basil leaves. Drizzle with remaining vinaigrette, and sprinkle pistachio nuts over.

Clemson Blue Cheese Ice Cream

Servings: 16

5 cups	Half and half	1 cup	Clemson Blue Cheese
1 cup	Honey	1 tsp	Salt to taste
2 cups	Egg yolk		

In a large sauce pot bring half and half and honey to a boil, and remove from the heat. Pour egg yolks into a small mixing bowl, stir a little of the cream mixture into it, and then add all of the egg mixture into the cream. Add Clemson Blue Cheese and salt. Chill before pouring into the ice cream maker. Proceed according to your ice cream maker's instructions. TIP: Serve with pears poached in red wine and port-wine reduction

Clemson Blue Cheese and Chocolate Ice Cream

Servings: 16

5 cups	Half and half	1 cup	Clemson Blue Cheese, crumbled
1 cup	Honey	2 cups	Egg yolk
2 ounces	Dark chocolate, shaved		

In a sauce pot, heat half and half, and honey until simmering. Pour egg yolks into a mixing bowl, and ladle hot cream over them. Stir continuously. Add Clemson Blue Cheese and chill. Pour chilled mixture into an ice cream maker. Churn according to manufacturer's instructions. When mixture is thick and creamy, add chocolate shavings. Continue freezing for 2 minutes. Pour finished ice cream into a freezer-friendly container and store. TIP: Serve with poached pears.

TASTES OF CLEMSON BLUE CHEESE

Breads

ABC Quick Bread
Servings: 24 / Yield: 2 loafs

1 cup	Unsalted butter		2 tsp	Baking soda
2 cups	Sugar		¼ cup	Unsweetened cocoa powder
4	Eggs		1 cup	Sour cream
3 cups	Clemson Blue Cheese crumbles		1 cup	Semi-sweet chocolate chips
2 tsp	Vanilla extract		1 cup	Toasted sliced almonds
3 cups	All-purpose flour			

In a mixing bowl, cream together butter, sugar, and eggs. Add Clemson Blue Cheese and vanilla. Sift in flour, baking soda, and cocoa powder; mix well and blend in sour cream, chocolate chips, and almonds. Pour into 2 lightly greased loaf pans (9 x 5), and bake in a 325-degree oven for 1 hour.

Hazelnut and Clemson Blue Cheese Shortbread
Servings: 16 / Yield: 32

8 ounces	Clemson Blue Cheese, crumbled, room temperature		¼ tsp	Cayenne pepper
			½ cup	Cornstarch
4 ounces	Butter, room temperature		⅔ cup	Hazelnuts, shelled, toasted and
1 cup	All-purpose flour			finely chopped with skin removed

In a mixing bowl or food processor, combine Clemson Blue Cheese and butter. Add flour, cornstarch, and cayenne pepper. Mix until it resembles coarse meal. Add hazelnuts and mix until moist clumps form. Place the dough on a sheet of plastic wrap, and work the dough until it holds together. Shape dough into a log, wrap in plastic wrap, and refrigerate for a minimum of 1 hour. Cut log into ¼-inch slices, and place them on a sheet pan with parchment paper. Bake at 325F until light brown on bottom (about 15 minutes). Remove from oven and let cool on rack.
TIP: Alternatively, serve with a dollop of sour cream or cream cheese on top.

Clemson Blue Cheese Biscuits
Servings: 12 / Yield: 12

4 cups	All-purpose flour		4 ounces	Butter
4 tsp	Baking powder		6 ounces	Clemson Blue Cheese, crumbled
1 tsp	Baking soda		1 cup	Milk
½ tsp	Salt			

Sift flour, baking powder, baking soda, and salt into a large mixing bowl. Work the butter into the flour mixture, and add 5 ounces of the Clemson Blue Cheese. Blend, add milk, and mix well until it forms soft dough. Place dough on a floured table, and roll out to ¾-inch thickness; cut into 2-inch rounds. Place rounds on a greased baking sheet, and top each with a little of the remaining Clemson Blue Cheese. Bake at 425F for 10 to 12 minutes until risen and golden brown.

Clemson Blue Cheese Muffins ▶
Yield: 16

2 cups	Flour	½ cup	Oil
1 cup	Sugar	½ cup	Water
½ Tbsp	Baking powder	1 tsp	Vanilla extract
½ Tbsp	Cinnamon	½ cup	Walnuts, chopped
3	Eggs	1 cup	Clemson Blue Cheese crumbles

In a mixing bowl, combine flour, sugar, baking powder, and cinnamon. In another bowl, combine eggs, oil, water, and vanilla extract. Fold the flour mixture into the egg mixture. Add walnuts and Clemson Blue Cheese. Mix just enough to incorporate. Divide into buttered muffin pans, and bake at 400F for 20 to 25 minutes or until done.

Clemson Blue Cheese and Scallion Scones
Servings: 12 / Yield: 12

2 cups	All-purpose flour	3	Scallions, thinly sliced
1 Tbsp	Baking powder	1 large	Egg
½ tsp	Ground white pepper	¾ cup	Half and half
4 ounces	Clemson Blue Cheese, crumbled		

In a large mixing bowl, combine flour, baking powder, and white pepper. Add Clemson Blue Cheese and scallions, and mix all ingredients together. In a small bowl, beat egg and half and half to blend. Stir egg mixture into dry ingredients, and mix until dough forms. Divide dough in half, and on a lightly floured table, flatten each piece into ¾-inch-thick round. Cut each round into 6 wedges. Transfer wedges to a baking sheet, and bake at 375F for about 25 minutes until tops are brown.

Three-Cheese Bread
Servings: 12

2 cups	All-purpose flour	1	Egg
1 Tbsp	Sugar	1 cup	Milk
1½ tsp	Baking powder	2 ounces	Clemson Blue Cheese, crumbled
1 tsp	Salt	2 Tbsp	Cheddar cheese, shredded
1 tsp	Dry mustard	2 Tbsp	Parmesan cheese, grated
¼ cup	Butter, cold		

In a large mixing bowl, combine flour, sugar, baking powder, salt, and dry mustard. Cut in butter until mixture gets crumbly. In a small mixing bowl, whip egg and milk together. Stir milk mixture into flour mixture until moistened and sticky. Fold in Clemson Blue Cheese, cheddar, and Parmesan cheeses. Mix well. Pour dough into a greased loaf pan (8 x 4), and bake at 325F oven for 45 to 50 minutes or until a toothpick inserted near the middle comes out clean. Cool for a few minutes before transferring to a wire rack.

Clemson Blue Cheese Focaccia
Servings: 8

2¾ cups	All-purpose flour	1 cup	Very warm water, (120F to 130F)
1 package	Rapid Rise Yeast	2 Tbsp	Olive oil
2½ tsp	Dried oregano leaves	1	Egg
½ tsp	Salt		

CLEMSON BLUE CHEESE AND WALNUT TOPPING:
¼ cup	Olive oil
¾ cup	Walnuts, chopped
½ cup	Clemson Blue Cheese, crumbled

In large bowl, combine 1½ cups flour, undissolved yeast, oregano, and salt. Stir very warm water and oil into dry ingredients. Stir in egg and enough remaining flour to make stiff batter. Cover; let rest 10 minutes. With lightly oiled hands, spread batter in oiled baking pan (13 × 9). Spread with Clemson Blue Cheese and walnut topping. Cover loosely with plastic wrap, and let rise in warm, draft-free place until almost doubled in size, about 15 to 30 minutes. Bake at 400F for 25 minutes or until done. Cool in pan on wire rack.

CLEMSON BLUE CHEESE AND WALNUT TOPPING: Drizzle ¼ cup olive oil over batter. Sprinkle with ¾ cup chopped walnuts and ½ cup (2 ounces) crumbled Clemson Blue Cheese; press nuts into batter.

Clemson Blue Cheese Bread
Servings: 12

2	Italian bread loaves	8 ounces	Butter, softened
10 ounces	Clemson Blue Cheese, crumbled	2 ounces	Parmesan cheese, grated

Cut bread loafs in half lengthwise. In a small mixing bowl or in a food processor, blend Clemson Blue Cheese and butter until smooth. Broil bread, cut-side up until crisp. Spread cheese mixture over cut side of bread, and sprinkle with Parmesan cheese. Return it to the broiler and broil until cheese bubbles and begins to brown. Cut bread into 1-inch slices and serve.

Clemson Blue Cheese Baguette
Servings: 10

1	French baguette	3 ounces	Clemson Blue Cheese, crumbled
3 ounces	Butter, softened	2 ounces	Boursin cheese

Cut bread into ¾-inch-thick slices (but not all the way through) leaving slices attached at the bottom. In a small mixing bowl, combine butter, Clemson Blue Cheese, and Boursin cheese. Spread cheese mixture between bread slices. Wrap bread tightly in a large piece of aluminum foil. Bake in a 375-degree oven for 10 minutes or until bread is toasted and heated through. Serve warm.

Sandwiches

Caramelized Onion, Pear, and Clemson Blue Cheese
    Panini 50
Chicken and Clemson Blue Cheese Salad Croissant 49
Clemson Blue Cheese Vegetable Pizza Sandwich 49
Roast Beef and Clemson Blue Cheese Sandwich 49
Turkey and Clemson Blue Cheese Baguette Sandwich 51
Turkey and Tomato Cobb Wrap 50

Seafood

Clemson Blue Cheese Baked Mahi-Mahi 53
Clemson Blue Cheese Baked Shrimp 52
Flounder with Spinach, Pine Nuts, and
    Clemson Blue Cheese 52
Shrimp, Clemson Blue Cheese, and Grits 52

Poultry

Bacon-wrapped Chicken Breast with Cashews and
    Clemson Blue Cheese 54
Chicken with Shiitake and Clemson Blue Cheese Sauce 55
Sautéed Chicken Breast with Creamy
    Clemson Blue Cheese Sauce 54

Meat

Beef Tips in Beer and Clemson Blue Cheese 56
Clemson Blue Cheese Pork Chops 57
Clemson Blue Cheese Burgers 62
Clemson Blue Cheese Meatballs 59
Clemson Blue Cheese Stuffed Steak with Mushrooms 57
Clemson Blue Cheese Tenderloin Steaks 59
Clemson Cheeseburgers with Pancetta 60
Creamy Clemson Blue Cheese Bacon Burgers 57
Grilled Clemson Blue Cheese Lamb Patties 62
Meatloaf with Buffalo Sauce and Clemson Blue Cheese 56
New York Strip Steaks with Clemson Blue Cheese 59
Oven-Roasted Pork Loin with Clemson Blue
    Cheese Sauce 60
Pan-Roasted Strip Steak over Clemson Blue
    Cheese Onions 62
Ribeye Steaks with Clemson Blue Cheese and
    Blueberry Vinaigrette 60
The Blue Tiger Burger 61

Pasta

Buffalo Chicken Lasagna 66
Buffalo Chicken Pasta 66
Clemson Blue Cheese Fettuccine 65
Fettuccine with Pancetta and Clemson Blue Cheese 67
Linguine with Prosciutto Ham and Clemson Blue Cheese 65
Mac and Clemson Blue Cheese 65
Orzo with Caramelized Onions and Clemson Blue Cheese 63
Orzo with Cherry Tomatoes, Herbs and
    Clemson Blue Cheese 63
Potato and Clemson Blue Cheese Ravioli 63

Egg Dishes

Bacon and Clemson Blue Cheese Quiche 69
Egg Sandwich with Bacon, Arugula, and
    Clemson Blue Cheese 70
Eggs Baked with Clemson Blue Cheese 69
Eggs Bleudict 70
Ham and Clemson Blue Cheese Omelet 69
Sausage and Clemson Blue Cheese Casserole 70
Scrambled Eggs with Clemson Blue Cheese and Chives 71

Vegetables and Side Dishes

Baked Chipotle and Clemson Blue Cheese Grits 74
Baked Mashed Sweet Potatoes with Bacon and
    Clemson Blue Cheese 77
Baked Sweet Potato with Crumbled Clemson Blue Cheese 74
Cauliflower Fritters with Clemson Blue Cheese Sauce 74
Clemson Blue Cheese and Rosemary Potatoes 78
Clemson Blue Cheese Au Gratin Potatoes 73
Clemson Blue Cheese Baked Tomatoes 73
Clemson Blue Cheese Stuffing 78
Honey Glazed Carrots with Clemson Blue Cheese 78
Potato and Clemson Blue Cheese Casserole 77
Potatoes in Clemson Blue Cheese Cream 79
Roasted Clemson Blue Cheese Potatoes 78
Scalloped Sweet Potatoes with Leeks and
    Clemson Blue Cheese 73
Sweet Potatoes with Walnuts and Clemson Blue Cheese 77
Twice-Baked Clemson Blue Cheese Potato 76

Desserts

Apple Pie with Clemson Blue Cheese 83
Baked Pears with Pecans and Clemson Blue Cheese 81
Clemson Blue Cheese and Chocolate Ice Cream 85
Clemson Blue Cheese Baked Apples with Pecans 83
Clemson Blue Cheese Bread Pudding 84
Clemson Blue Cheesecake with Walnuts 81
Clemson Blue Cheese Ice Cream 85
Clemson Blue Cheese Soufflé 83
Clemson Blue Cheese, Green Peppercorn, and
    Brandy Cheesecake 81
Clemson Blue Cheese with Marinated Strawberries and
    Pistachio Nuts 84
No-Bake Savory Clemson Blue Cheesecake 84

Breads

ABC Quick Bread 87
Clemson Blue Cheese and Scallion Scones 88
Clemson Blue Cheese Baguette 89
Clemson Blue Cheese Biscuits 87
Clemson Blue Cheese Bread 89
Clemson Blue Cheese Focaccia 89
Clemson Blue Cheese Muffins 89
Hazelnut and Clemson Blue Cheese Shortbread 87
Three-Cheese Bread 88

Christian Thormose

BORN IN ODENSE, DENMARK, Christian graduated from culinary school and finished as a four-year apprentice at Søllerød Kro, Søllerød. He then served as a sergeant in the Danish army. Christian's work as a cook, sous-chef, and executive chef has taken him to Denmark, France, and the United States, where he has delighted restaurant goers, hotel guests, and private-club members. For more than 10 years, he worked as an executive chef and food production manager for Aramark at Clemson University. In 2008, he was chosen as a chef for the 2008 Summer Olympics in Beijing and traveled in 2012 to work the Summer Olympics in London.

CPSIA information can be obtained
at www.ICGtesting.com
Printed in the USA
JSHW021628071219
2858JS00001B/1

9 781942 954583